BROOKLANDS
BOOKS

W9-CGS-218

THUNDERBIRD

1955·1957

Compiled by
R.M. Clarke

ISBN 0 946489 79 3

Distributed by
Brooklands Book Distribution Ltd.
'Holmerise', Seven Hills Road,
Cobham, Surrey, England
Printed in Hong Kong

BROOKLANDS BOOKS

CONTENTS

BROOKLANDS BOOKS

ACKNOWLEDGEMENTS

On a recent visit to the great Automobile Club of America meeting at Hershey, I was struck by the fine turnout of Thunderbird two-seaters. These cars appealed to my European up-bringing as they were restrained in design and not over adorned with chrome bric-a-brac.

Some time later, in search of more information on the marque I acquired Richard Langworth's enjoyable book "The Thunderbird Story: Personal Luxury". This provided an insight to Ford's objectives at that time with regard to a sporting car and then for good measure went on to tell how in 1958 it gained a thousand pounds and grew into a four seater.

The outcome of all this is the book you are holding. Some very enjoyable weeks have been spent researching and reading these stories and I hope that the articles that have been selected will prove to be of value to today's owners and restorers of these "classy machines".

If you like starting a book with a good factual introduction, please turn immediately to page 93 where Frank Taylor reveals all about the Thunderbird in his comprehensive article for Car Classics 'Three years of Glory'.

Brooklands Books are printed in small numbers and now with over 300 titles are one of the main works of reference for auto enthusiasts. We exist because firstly there is a thirst for information and secondly because the leading publishers of the world's major magazines generously support us by allowing us to include their copyright stories. We are in debted in this instance to the publishers of Auto Age, Autocar, Autosport, Car Classics, Car Life, Model Review, Motor Life, Motor Trend, Road & Track, Speed Age, Sports Cars Illustrated and Wheels for their understanding and ongoing help.

R.M. Clarke

NEW FORD SPORTS CAR IS A

Thunderin' Thunderbird

By Don MacDonald

PERHAPS THE OUTSTANDING feature of the new Ford Thunderbird is the clever wedding of sports car functionalism with American standards of comfort. Rather than be first in the field, much was gained by a period of watchful waiting, typical of shrewd L. D. Crusoe, Ford Motor Co. V.P. and general manager of Ford Division. Before deciding to go into competition with Corvette and the KD-161, Crusoe insisted on a full-sized, all-metal car whose major parts would be interchangable with a stock Ford.

The stock Ford we're talking about, of course, is not the *current* stock model *but the one planned for 1955.* With the exception of hood and grille, the Thunderbird is an accurate prediction of things to come from Dearborn, even to the wraparound windshield.

These first pictures are of a prototype made entirely of clay (except for tires, some trim, and glass). The production version will be made of metal rather than Fiberglas, which is indicative of anticipated sales volume. Besides the removable plastic top (optional), there will be a hand-operated canvas top folding neatly out of sight under a metal boot.

Ford has stolen a jump on its competitors in the sports car field by specifying roll-up windows with power lifts optional. The instrument panel contains Ford's legible Astrodome speedometer along with a 5000-rpm tach and sweep-second clock. The steering column telescopes in or out three inches to fit all size drivers.

Neck-snapping performance through either Fordomatic or standard transmission (both floor-shifted) is guaranteed by the Interceptor engine (160 bhp at 4400 rpm). With a curb weight of 2800 pounds, our slide rule shows that the Thunderbird should be about 50 car lengths ahead of a conventional Ford from a standing start in 40 seconds. The 256-cubic-inch engine (essentially a Mercury) is the same one used in Ford's police cars. These employ a four-barrel carburetor with its own inlet vacuum to actuate the secondary venturis.

From the rear, you can see the dual exhausts protruding from the bumper guards. Suspension is standard leaf springs in the rear with Ford ball-joint in front. Although the car is nearly a foot lower than a current Ford sedan, road clearance (5.5 inches) is only slightly less.

5

AUTO REVIEW

FORD
THUNDERBIRD

Ford's proud entry into the American sport-car field, the new Thunderbird, a sleek, low model with room in the front seat for a third passenger. Under wraps for a year and a half, it's in production with deliveries scheduled for fall.

CAR LIFE STAFF REPORT

BEST kept secret the automobile industry has nurtured in years has now come smoothly out of Dearborn—Ford's new sport car, the Thunderbird.

Rumors were barely audible some forty-five days before the cleanly designed production made its appearance on February 19 in Detroit. April's CAR LIFE conjectured on it in copy written in early February; predicted that it would be a Ford, rather than a Mercury.

It had been under wraps almost eighteen months and was actually planned for 1955 production. Introductory photos from a rear quarter view show a 1955 plate on the back license rack.

Fall deliveries unofficially are predicted at a price reported to be only slightly over $3,000—well under Chevrolet's Corvette and Kaiser's sport car.

Until two weeks before its debut, Ford hadn't definitely decided on a name. Offi-

Two Thunderbird models are available, with removable hardtop or folding top which folds out of sight behind seat. Thunderbird is full-sized but a foot lower than a Ford sedan.

Surprised by the 1955 plate? Ford intended to spring the Thunderbird next year, but decided to put it into production for delivery this fall.

cials hadn't even decided to refer to it as a "sport" car.

But on February 17, L. W. Smead, Ford's general sales manager told a full-scale press conference all about it.

"The Thunderbird," he said with pardonable pride, "is a new kind of sport car.

"We are convinced it will set a new trend in the automobile industry. It provides all of the comforts, conveniences and all-weather protection available in any of today's modern automobiles."

Mr. Smead may very well be oh, so right.

It is powered by a 160-hp., Y-block, V-8 engine, has ball-joint front suspension and offers Fordomatic, overdrive or standard transmission.

Side windows are roll up, the steering wheel can be telescoped three inches to agree with the driver's height and reach; power steering, power brakes, power-lift windows and powered seat are among the optionals.

Biggest selling point over other sport cars, other than the obvious attributes:

It will seat a third person.

It is all-metal, with Ford components available at virtually any Ford dealer.

It may be purchased with a special composition hardtop which turns it into an all-weather automobile. The convertible cloth top folds completely out of sight behind the seat.

The Thunderbird is full-sized, but a foot lower in over-all height than a stock Ford sedan. It is 175 inches long on a 102-inch wheelbase; stands 51½ inches tall.

Engineered as a high-performance vehicle, the engine has the latest short-stroke, low-friction design with 256 cubic inch displacement, a four-barrel carburetor and dual exhausts coming out of bumper ports.

On or off, a special plastic hardtop makes the Thunderbird an all-weather car. It is easily removed or put back in place. Roll-up windows fit tightly.

Test engineers say that from a standing start, in forty seconds the Thunderbird will be fifty-three car lengths out in front of a 1954 conventional car.

In addition to normal instruments, the Thunderbird has a tachometer.

The high fender line sweeps backward in a straight line and is slightly lower at the tail fins than at the headlights. The door tops are only 33.7 inches from the ground. The low hood line is accentuated by an air scoop that extends from the windshield forward over the oil-bath air cleaner.

The oval-shaped grille is covered with bright metal square mesh. Two round bumper guards rise from the wedge-shaped bumper with a center spinner in each guard to retain the traditional Ford grille design. Two circular parking lamps are located in the fenders directly below the headlamps.

Ford's news bureau pulled all stops in explaining origin of the name—Thunderbird.

The Thunderbird, known to American Indians as an omen of good luck, is a mythical bird supposed to cause thunder, lightning and rain. It symbolizes, among many things, "power, swiftness and prosperity."

It was called the helper of man because, by flapping its wings, it was believed to cause thunder and lightning and bring rain to the parched fields.

"No man," say the Indians, "can see the Thunderbird except in flashes as it flies swiftly through the clouds with arrows of lightning bolts tucked beneath its wings."

Mr. Smead put it this way:

"We are introducing the Thunderbird at the Detroit Auto Show as an outstanding example of the kind of forward planning that is going on at Ford division. The car has been under development for many months as the re-

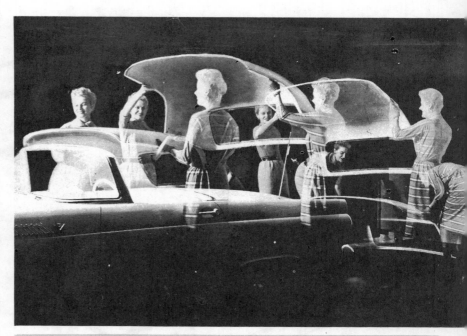

One, two, three, four . . . two persons can take off or replace the Thunderbird's hardtop in a matter of seconds. Automatic holds keep top firmly in position.

sult of substantial public demand for a distinctively different, American-made, high-performance vehicle.

"Because of this demand, we saw no point in keeping good news a secret and we decided to introduce the car at this time."

Allowing for normal tooling time, he said, "we intend to get into production later this year at Dearborn, and the car will be on sale at Ford dealers in the fall.

He said they are not announcing the

Thunderbird's price at this time, "but we can say that its basic price will not exceed the basic price of other cars in the same field."

Prospective buyers are already sending up a fervent hope that the latitude provided in such a nebulous price discussion won't permit up-grading. Advance notices of the Kaiser and Chevrolet sport models talked promisingly of "about $3,000" before actual sales came. They wound up on the showroom floor a lot nearer $3,500 than $3,000.   ☆☆

Ford

THUNDERBIRD

Luxury cockpit of Ford's new "personal" car.

THE FIRST truly American "personal" car is the way the Ford Motor Company describes their new 2/3 seater, high-performance, Thunderbird model scheduled for its first public showing late in October.

To the purist the Thunderbird has far too much luxury to qualify as a sports car, but even *that* group will find much of interest in the specifications of this car. The design concept alone proves that, for included in the list of desiderata were such items as high performance, good handling, quick steering, firm suspension and good brakes.

How the above sports car features have been combined with passenger car comfort, safety and convenience is our story. The Thunderbird has a wheelbase of 102 inches, weighs 3147 lbs. at the curb. The V-8 engine is 15% larger than the current Mercury, and while no horsepower figures have been re-

leased, something like 190 bhp can be expected. The resultant ratio of 16.6 lbs/bhp insures high performance, even by competition sports car standards.

Good handling qualities may come by accident, by long evolution, or by good design and thorough testing. The Thunderbird falls into the latter category and its design features include a weight distribution of 52/48, ball joint front suspension, a 3-piece ride stabilizer, and rubber bumpers to reduce rear spring "wind-up" during fast acceleration. The steering gear ratio is given as 20 to 1, (equivalent to about 3.7 turns lock to lock). As is well known, good handling with independent front suspension requires an extremely rigid frame and the Thunderbird's frame has box section side rails, four cross members and an I-beam type X-member.

Continued on page 52

Underhood space with a V-8 is at a premium.

The Ford Thunderbird undergoing rough treatment on a special staggered-bump test road.

Ford's New Sports Contender

Here are the first road impressions of American Ford's new semi-sports car. It will not be available in Australia.

FORD have released the Thunderbird, their answer to Chevrolet's Corvette. This car, called a "personal" car by Ford and a "sports car" by the man in the street, is a transition between the stock model American car and the imported sports car.

Frank Rowsome, one of the editors of "Popular Science," was the first man outside the company to drive the new car. In this special feature he gives us his impressions.

* * *

The word on the new Ford Thunderbird (the high-performance car that Ford partly unveiled last March, and which will be formally announced this month) is that it is some car—able, good-looking, and, if you wish, sinfully luxurious.

The Bird moves more rapidly than you will generally find it advisable to conduct it; it foots creditably around turns that would carry most U.S. cars through the fence; it also provides such amenities, conspicuously lacking in its trans-Atlantic sports sisters, as real weather protection, considerable luggage space and non-contorted entrance and exit.

Certain points should be ticked off on the other side. It won't be cheap—the guesses hit around 3,200 dollars, depending on optional equipment. (An M.G. costs around 2,200 dollars in the U.S.).

It isn't designed for the man who has a houseful of kids—it will seat three, but the man who draws the middle should have short legs to match. Finally, it has characteristics that will distress sports car cultists: 3,147 pound curb weight, 20 to 1 steering ratio and plenty of such optional concessions for the ladies as an automatic gearbox, power steering and power brakes.

Ford engineers know that these aspects of the Bird will inflame die-hard sports-car characters. But they are not too concerned about it.

The car is good to drive. I got a crack at a Bird in July, the first non-company person, I was told, to be allowed to drive it. There were then only a handful of Birds in existence and the project engineers didn't want to let go. In return for a promise not to put a stop-watch on it and to do without some data that Ford wants to reserve for late advertising, I was permitted to drive it around some back roads.

Slide behind the wheel, which is more nearly vertical than in conventional cars, and lock it at the point in its three-inch fore-and-aft travel that feels best. Then work the rise-or-fall and to-or-fro controls of the seat (standard equipment) to please your anatomy.

If you've served much time on imported sports cars, you'll relish the shoulder and foot room. There is no feeling of having inserted your feet in a shrunken sleeping bag, no need to twist your right foot into bizarre deflections, and no difficulty in finding an ample parking space for the left one.

Fire up with the key-turn switch. You will like, I think, the music from the 4,783 c.c. engine.

The Bird that I drove had an automatic box with a stubby range selector jutting up from the left side of the drive-shaft hump. It travels in a straight fore-and-aft arc through the positions, reading, front to rear: Park, Reverse, Neutral, Drive and Low.

A thumb button on top releases a gate intended to discourage you from whanging it into reverse in an excess of enthusiasm. (Sometime when leisure permits, you may wish to muse on the oddity of designing an automatic's selector to imitate a genuine stick shift; it is a mysterious piece of associative merchandising.

Even case-hardened gear-shifters will grudgingly like one thing

New engine has a big shroud over the fan to help it draw air through the radiator. (Frank Rowsome has his hand on it.) Scoop in the bonnet feeds the four-barrel carburettor with cool air.

The Thunderbird engine, a V8, has 95 mm. bore, 84 mm. stroke and a capacity of 4,783 c.c. Compression ratio is 8 to 1. Other features are a four-barrel carburettor, dual exhausts and a three-speed transmission as standard. Overdrive or automatic transmission are available as extras.

FORDS NEW SPORTS CONTENDER

they've done to the automatic transmission. Move it to Drive, put your foot down and you'll light out with a zip that no automatic in Drive has ever given you before.

Don't try it on anything but a smooth hard-top road—even so, you'll get a moment or so of wheelspin screech. The take-off is similar but brisker than an automatic that's started in Low and then moved to Drive.

Ordinary Ford and Mercury automatics currently start in intermediate and upshift to high range. The Bird's automatic does this, too, so long as you don't flatten it. But open the throttle wide at the start, or at any speed up to about 14 miles an hour, and the transmission instantly engages Low and pushes you back against the foam-rubber seats. Exact acceleration figures are officially secret, but a Bird might do 0-60 in 10 sec.

The car has a capable, alert feel. The springing is firm but not unpleasant; on a beat-up concrete road the expansion joints thrum at you, but don't give teeth rattle.

On turns it stays flat and slides or holds with a light touch of wheel or throttle. We found a gently-curving dirt road where I learned that the Bird is willing to slide with cool precision. Finally, the Ford man promised cruel and unusual punishment if we bent the car, so we headed for home.

The top speed is currently one of Ford's darker secrets, but you can expect around 119.

That 20-to-1 steering ratio is going to be criticised. Project engineers say defensively that it is an easy "transitional step" down from the stock Ford's 25.3-to-1 ratio.

When you point out that many stock sedans have ratios as quick or quicker than the Bird's it is explained that the car was not designed purely from scratch, but was intended to use as many production parts as possible, and 20-to-1 was about as low as that gear could be pushed without upsetting the steering geometry.

When the Bird was first shown to the public last March the power plant was to be an overhead-valve, 160 h.p. V-8 of 4,200 cubic inches.

Although Ford officials denied it, this was clearly the 1954 Mercury engine in false whiskers. At the projected curb weight of 2,833 pounds, this first engine gave the Bird a power loading of 17.7 pounds per horsepower, comfortably ahead of the Chevrolet Corvette's 19 pounds, and almost identical with the Jaguar XK 120's 17.8 pounds.

Later it became apparent that production Thunderbirds would run several hundred pounds heavier—and that future Corvettes would probably get a hotted-up version of Chevrolet's spanking new V-8, due at the end of this month. So Ford's decision, made early this summer, was to put a big 4,783 c.c. engine in the Bird.

Rated horsepower is another of Ford's secrets, but it is a reasonable inference that the new inches will add some 20 h.p. to begin with to the original 160.

Newest member of the Ford family of o.h.v. engines, this one has a 95 mm. bore and 84 mm. stroke, a four-barrel carburettor and dual exhausts. The cooling system includes a big shroud around the fan and a special radiator, not borrowed from Ford or Merc, that is pressurised at 13-15 pounds, twice the normal amount.

A manual-shift transmission will be standard, with overdrive or automatic as options. The axle ratios are 3.73 for manual, 3.90 for overdrive and 3.31 for the automatic. Clutch and brake pedals are the suspended kind.

The Bird uses Hotchkiss drive, with five-leaf rear springs. Special rubber bumpers are mounted over strategic parts of the springs to prevent the spring from being bowed upward during fast acceleration. Front suspension is Ford's ball-joint system.

The brakes are duo-servo hydraulics with 191 square inches of lining area. Because of the 102-inch wheelbase the frame couldn't be borrowed, but had to be designed from scratch. It is a double-drop job with an "I"-beam cross-piece and four cross members.

Among the numerous fancy touches, not all standard equipment, are sensuous vinyl upholstery combinations, push-button doors, a detachable and insulated plastic hardtop, sound and heat insulation, arm rests, heater, radio and a sweep second hand on the clock.

Certain developments can be predicted:

● There will be turmoils and agitations about what the Bird is. Ford will not succeed in its efforts to have it dubbed a "personal car"; the public will serenely call it "that Ford sports car," and a little core of imported-car enthusiasts will stay awake nights thinking up supercilious comments.

● Although there will be virtual unanimity that the Bird isn't a competition car, single-minded owners will strip off several hundred pounds of comfort and do all right. Others won't try this, but will engage in casual highway scraps with such cocks-of-the-walk as Caddy, Lincoln, Corvette, Austin-Healey 100 and XK 120 Jag. The Bird should be able to hold or beat them.

"Turn right at the next scream!"

FORD *Thunderbird*

THE thunderbird is a creature in Indian mythology that symbolizes "power, swiftness and prosperity." We can't vouch for the prosperity, but there is little doubt that anyone owning a Ford Thunderbird, come next fall, will certainly have both power and swiftness. And along with these attributes this car bears the distinction of being the first 1955 model revealed to the public.

The Thunderbird is a new kind of car that has certain sports car characteristics but retains most of the comforts so dear to the American heart.

It has a folding cloth top but offers in addition a lightweight composition hardtop that can be removed and left at home. Roll-up windows are standard with optional power lifts.

Exhilarating performance should result from the 160 h.p. V-8 equipped with four-barrel carburetor and dual exhausts (essentially a Mercury engine), and a weight of 2837 lbs., about 400 lbs. less than stock models. Ford engineers say that "from a standing start, in 40 seconds the Thunderbird will be 53 car lengths out in front of a conventional 1954 car."

L. D. Crusoe, Ford vice president, said the car, which has an all-steel body, will be placed in production next fall. " . . .

most of the (Thunderbird's) major parts are interchangeable with our regular line of cars," he continued. "It is completely engineered and built so it can be serviced by any Ford dealer."

A clever and very practical innovation on this car is the seating arrangement. It is a kind of combination bench and bucket seat that is tailored to normally accommodate two persons, but provides a flat area between the two seating positions that will let a third passenger ride comfortably.

The wrap-around windshield, introduced on GM 1954 models apparently is here to stay and shows up on the Thunderbird. This, combined with the sloping hood should afford excellent forward vision. An air scoop on the hood channels air to the carburetor.

The new model can be purchased with power steering, power brakes and four-way power seat. It has an adjustable steering column which telescopes in or out three inches to fit all drivers. In addition to the normal instruments on the control panel, the Thunderbird has a tachometer to indicate engine r.p.m.

Its high fender line sweeps backward in a straight line and is slightly lower at the tail fins than at the headlights. The door tops are 33.7 inches from the ground and overall height is 51.5 inches. This is nearly a foot lower than the 1954 Ford sedan.

Frontal design of the Thunderbird is very neat,' with a nearly-full-width oval grille covered with square mesh. The presence of two round bumper guards protruding from the bumper is the only disturbing factor. Two similar bumper guards at the rear serve as outlets for the dual exhausts. Massive 8-inch tail lights dominate the rear end.

Gear shift lever for either the automatic transmission or standard transmission is in the floor. As on standard Ford cars, clutch and brake pedals are suspended from the dash.

The Thunderbird has a 102-inch wheelbase, 58-inch front and 56-inch rear tread. Its overall length is 175.5 inches. ★

SPECIFICATIONS
Ford Thunderbird

ENGINE

Type	V-8, O.H.V.
Bore and stroke	3.62" x 3.10"
Piston displacement	256 cu. in.
Compression ratio	7.5:1
Brake horsepower	160 h.p. @ 4400 r.p.m.
Carburetor	4-barrel
Exhaust system	dual mufflers and tail pipes

GENERAL

Transmission	conventional or automatic
Front suspension	coil spring independent with ball joints
Rear suspension	leaf springs
Weight, unladen	2837 lbs.

DIMENSIONS

Wheelbase	102 in.
Tread, front	58 in.
Tread, rear	56 in.
Overall length	175.5 in.
Overall height	51.5 in.

An optional, easy-to-handle, glass-fiber hardtop can
be locked into place—to give you winter-long comfort.

Coming your way...the new

What will the horsepower be? How fast
will it accelerate? What are the
cornering and ride characteristics?
When will it be on display?

A fabric top whisks into place in seconds—to protect you from
sudden rainstorms. It's completely out of sight when not in use.

SPORTS CAR

Ford THUNDERBIRD

The sleek, long, low lines of the Thunderbird...the sweeping, contoured windshield say distinction in every detail.

We can't answer *all* of your questions about the Thunderbird, yet. But we can give you *some* of the facts.

The power plant is a special edition of Ford's famous short-stroke, overhead-valve Y-block V-8. It will have an 8.1 to 1 compression ratio ... 292 cubic-inch displacement and 3.75 in. bore by 3.30 in. stroke. There will be a 4-barrel carburetor, dual exhausts and a special pressure-type cooling system.

The Thunderbird will also have Ford's Ball-Joint Front Suspension for the smoothest, most road-suiting ride you've ever experienced in a sports car. This feature and the Thunderbird's low center of gravity (it's just over a yard high from head to tread) make it hold the corners like a coat of paint.

It has many other features, some of which are usually associated with sports cars—others that are not. The Astra-Dial Control Panel includes a tachometer, signal lights for oil and generator, a clock with a sweep second hand, plus the standard instruments and controls. The steering wheel telescopes in or out a full three inches. Windows *roll* up. Luggage space is ample. The extra-wide, one-piece seat is foam rubber cushioned. *And the body is all-steel.* In addition, you can have all of Ford's optional power assists: power steering, brakes, windows and a *4-way* power seat ... Overdrive or Fordomatic.

Keep in touch with your Ford Dealer—"T" Day's coming soon!

Heel-over gives evidence of good ride, ability to stick in turns without drifting over line. Speed here was 55 mph

THE ACCUSATION that American car manufacturers couldn't build a sports car—even if they tried—is no longer valid. The first indication was the Chevrolet Corvette. And although the Ford Motor Co. is the first one to deny it, they have a *sports car* in the Thunderbird, and it's a good one.

Ford prefers to call it a "personal car." The thinking behind this, as brought out in a discussion with W. R. Burnett, Chief Passenger Car Engineer for Ford, is that "although the Thunderbird has the performance and attributes of most sports cars, management also felt that it should have a few more comforts to make it more appealing to a wider segment of the public." Besides having the power-operated four-way seat (which is actually for making the car usable for more people of varying builds and heights, rather than just comfort), the Thunderbird has power steering (optional) for more ease in city driving, power brakes, and complete weather protection in the form of a standard Fiberglas hardtop (that can be placed over the optional soft top when it's folded up behind the seat), and roll-up windows (power optional). This follows our thinking about the new type of sports car. You'll recall that we pointed out at the time of Thunderbird introduction (June MT), "The pattern [of sports car acceptance in this country] became evident. America was definitely interested in a *personal* car that was *fun to drive* and *feasible to own.*"

Enough for that. The car's been kicking around long enough for almost everyone to know most of the stories about it (except some of the finer points we're going to bring out here). So let's get on to the hottest news about the car. Wot'll she do? To find out, Don MacDonald and I visited the Ford Proving Ground (Dearborn, Mich.) on one spottily sunny day in be-

tween two rainy ones. Having the car for the better part of the afternoon enabled us to become familiar with it quickly.

Vision over the low hood is good, although there is a slight amount of distortion in the corners of the wrap-around windshield. With top up you feel pretty closed in, mostly because it's not like most of the new car "glass bowls."

All instruments (including a tach) are well-positioned and easy to read. Of interest to rally drivers is the sweep-second clock. The emergency brake is up under the dash, like passenger cars, instead of being "fly-off" *à la* sports cars. The foot pedals are far enough apart so that you don't get your feet tangled. You don't even have to reach across the wide bench-type seat to raise or lower the passenger's window, if you pay the extra loot for power-operation of it.

After getting it out on the grounds and getting acclimated to the car (with a Ford engineer beside me), I began to put it through its paces. The more I drove it, the more I liked it. The happiest thing to me was not that it could burn rubber from a standstill (which it will), nor that it can burn rubber when changing gears (even with a Fordomatic), nor that it feels so solid to driver and passenger alike, but—that it handles so superbly.

There's definite oversteer built into the car (which means that it will break loose in a turn before it drifts, unlike the true competition sports car). It hangs so well in the corners that you can take any given curve at 10-15 mph more than the '55 Ford (an improved version of the top handling car of '54). Most important is the feeling of security you get from the car. Ater pushing it around the handling course (asphalt, varying-radii turns) a few times I soon got confident enough to begin taking them at 55-65 mph. With more practice behind the wheel I felt sure that

I could up the speed—that's how the car impresses you.

With all of these good handling characteristics, the Thunderbird is also easy to drive, having an exceptionally short turning radius, a steering ratio of 20 to 1 (3.5 turns lock to lock, both with and without power steering). You can adjust the wheel to your own liking merely by loosening the adjustment on the column and pushing in or pulling out the wheel (three inches of movement).

The ride is unlike that which the die-hard sports car addict has come to expect from a sports car. It's firm enough to prevent too much bobbing coming out of a dip or flying over a bump, yet it's soft enough to be kind to a weak sacroiliac. There's a certain initial lean going through a corner, but it doesn't increase appreciably during severe cornering.

The standard power brakes make the Thunderbird squat down right now. Last year Ford brakes were among the best in their class, while the combination of larger brakes (11-inch drums instead of 10-inch) and the lighter weight make the Thunderbird brakes well above average.

Drag? Why not? The Thunderbird will go with the best of them, even with Fordomatic. Normally, a fast speed-shifter could outdrag an automatic car, but here's one case where they're even. After driving the Fordomatic job I had a chance to drive a couple with stick shifts. From first to second the gate wasn't exceptionally smooth, and though you can keep your foot down on the throttle all the way, it's asking a lot of the clutch, day-in and day-out. In shifting from second to third, you can keep your foot down and just "pop" the clutch. Going through this procedure, you'll wind up just about even with a Fordomatic 'Bird. Why? With Fordomatic, a hotter engine, rated at 198 horsepower, is used. The stick-shift engine has 190 hp.

FORD THUNDERBIRD

No car has caused so much conjecture as Ford's new Thunderbird. We looked for a lot, and when we drove it, we found it.

The Thunderbird's looks change considerably with its fender skirts removed

A time of 11 seconds is what we got for 0 to 60 mph, putting it into sports car company. The needle of the electric speedometer hit 80 mph just 19.4 seconds after the standing start. Axle "wind-up" is kept to a minimum by the use of rubber bumpers on the frame which the semi-elliptic rear springs contact on sudden take-offs before the springs distort too far.

Fordomatic for '55 now uses the low-gear starting feature (available on all '55 Ford products), which permits you to start in low gear instead of second by pushing the throttle all the way to the floor. It will then shift to second at about 30 mph, and to third gear around 60 mph. This is all accomplished while the selector is in DRIVE; it isn't necessary to use LOW, then to manually shift to DRIVE.

MT's Editor removes 'Bird's chrome air cleaner, exposing four-barrel carburetor; valve covers bear special insignia

Downshifts can be made to LOW at any speed. This puts you manually into second gear, then an automatic downshift to LOW comes at around 20 mph. Downshifts are considerably smoother.

The Fordomatic transmission lever, located above the driveshaft tunnel, is short and stubby (like that of most sports cars), giving you the feel of a conventional transmission. An interesting safety feature incorporated in the lever knob is a pushbutton lock on top of it to prevent inadvertent shifts from DRIVE to REVERSE or vice versa. You can go from LOW to DRIVE, but not through NEUTRAL into REVERSE unless you push the button.

Acceleration at passing speeds is impressive. We averaged times of 4.2 seconds to get from 30 to 50 mph, and 11 seconds from 50 to 80 mph. That's enough to indicate that the 'Bird meets its advertising claims of "sports car . . . performance."

Despite claims to the contrary, no-one outside of Ford personnel had tested the car for top-speed at presstime—and Ford people aren't talking. My guess, though (and I have reason to believe it's fairly accurate) is that it will fly along in the range of 120-mph-plus (if overdrive-equipped). That's as fast as most popular sports cars, or faster.

As I see it, the Ford Thunderbird has three basic points in its favor: a rakish, ground-hugging style; performance to match good sports cars; and a design that has built-in comfort for driver and passenger, with no penalty whatsoever to pay for their fun. It certainly seems like the right combination to make the car appealing to a fairly broad cross-section of the motoring public.

It takes two to do a quick, neat job of folding the Thunderbird's top down behind seat. Fiberglas hardtop is standard

Scanning Thunderbird's instrument layout, driver finds neat, legible setup with tach and clock straddling speedometer

Halfway up incline at the Ford Testing Grounds in Dearborn, one ML tester reaches out to show height of sill from pavement.

FORD
Thunderbird
ROAD TEST

*Not billed as a Sports Car,
Ford's new product
Accelerates, Corners, Rides
with the Best of Them.
Named after a Legend,
It may create One of its Own.*

MOTOR *Life* Test Staff Report

ALTHOUGH there have been many premature reports on the performance of Ford's new personal car, the nation's road testers can't seem to agree on their figures. It's not difficult to understand. In some cases, a quick spin around the block plus some stock publicity photos have been reported as "complete rundowns" on this new car. One able reporter indicated, sagely, that the car was "faster." What it was faster than was not observed. MOTOR *Life* has given the Thunderbird its standard road test. Here are the real facts about that car.

The Thunderbird or "T-Bird" as afficianados are already

nicknaming it, is a reality even if the suggested factory price of $2695 (including hardtop) still seems like a dream to the speculators who were "sure" that Ford couldn't produce it under $4,000, f.o.b. Detroit.

In a car market inundated with the idea that good high-performance cars should cost a lot of money, the T-Bird revolutionizes present thinking. The price of the Thunderbird hovers just around the price of a low-range convertible—but from that point on, the similarity stops. The Thunderbird, not advertised as a sports car by its creators, is very close to being one. A sports car, by definition, features excellent suspension and handling characteristics, top quality acceleration and top speed performance. A sports car has excellent power-to-weight ratio, trim, sleek lines, a dash and color not present in conventional cars plus a top-grade maneuverability in traffic and on the open road.

The Thunderbird does.

Road testing a product is generally accepted as routine, everyday work, not calculated to upset the entire office staff: circulation, bookkeeping, art, promotion and clerical departments. But the news of the Thunderbird road test brought restlessness to the MOTOR *Life* offices, first sight of the car brought trade-in ideas to nearly every member of the staff.

After driving the car, in Los Angeles and at the Ford proving grounds at Dearborn, the test staff is convinced that Ford planners will find no public apathy toward this car, that the entire "different" car movement will get a boost upstairs from the impetus of this car on the market.

Thunderbird offers adequate luggage capacity for sports-type car. Bumper guards house dual exhausts. Gas filler extends through lid.

Dashboard has flattened Ford speedometer, tachometer, clock with sweep-second hand, adjustable steering wheel and seat.

Power plant is 292 cubic inch ohv V-8 with single four-throat carburetor and dual exhausts. The Thunderbird exceeds 115 mph.

FORD THUNDERBIRD
Performance and Specifications

ACCELERATION

0-30 mph	4.30 seconds
0-60 mph	10.75 seconds

TOP SPEED

Fastest One-way	118 mph
Slowest One-way	115 mph

FUEL CONSUMPTION

Constant 30 mph	20.2 mpg

ENGINE—ohv V8. Bore and stroke: 3.75″ x 3.30″. Compression ratio, 8.5:1. Displacement, 292 cubic inches. Advertised horsepower, 190—conventional, 198—Fordomatic.

REAR AXLE RATIOS—Conventional transmission, 3.73:1. Overdrive, 3.92:1, Fordomatic, 3.31:1.

DIMENSIONS

Wheelbase	102 inches
Tread	56″ front and rear
Width, overall	70.1 inches
Height, overall	51.9 inches
Weight (shipping)	3225 pounds
Steering, turns lock to lock	3.5
Turning radius	36 feet

SPEEDOMETER ERROR

At 60 mph	Actual speed, 56.25 mph

FORD THUNDERBIRD ROAD TEST

No prophets on the test staff, we still feel that the Thunderbird will be highly successful. And for a very simple reason: it's the American version of a sports car, roll up windows and all.

Adjustment to the Thunderbird is simple; just look at it. Or drive it. Ford has done the rest. Inside the cockpit, there's a sports car feel which will be just a bit strange to true enthusiasts: it's comfortable. The 52″ wide seat will accommodate three on occasion, but has basically been designed for two passengers. The dashboard offers a real competition car feel to this roadster, it's complete with tachometer marked in hundreds, an electric clock with a sweep second hand (for do-it-yourself road testing or accurate trip logging) and a wide, flat speedometer. The steering wheel is adjustable in and out of the dash and is positioned upright for easier handling. Shift mechanism is located in a chrome gate on the tunnel and, in the Fordomatic model, the handle is complete with a thumb-push button to prevent accidental movement of the lever.

Both test cars were complete with all of the power accessories: radio, heater, four-way seat, Fordomatic, power steering and power brakes. Of that group, conventional equipment for the suggested $2695 price will include the fiberglass hardtop, four-way seat, plus standard equipment (generally considered optional) including roll up windows, dual exhausts, four barrel carburetor, tach and the aforementioned electric clock. As a surprise move, the soft top for the car is an accessory. Nearly every speculator assumed it would be the other way around. Ford has evidently found a way to produce fiberglass tops for less cost than the bows and fabric for the soft top. For California and other sections of the country where the rainy season arrives only when expected, a soft top won't be neces-

sary and the hardtop can be leaned against the garage door for months at a time.

The 102-inch wheelbase car stands but 51.9 inches high with the top in place, is powered by a 292 cu. inch V-8 block which turns out 198 (in Fordomatic models) horsepower. Front overhang is a mere 27 inches, but the rear overhang, in order to accommodate luggage space, goes up to almost 46 inches. Even at that,

the weight distribution of the car is a very fair 52% front/48% rear.

Included on Ford's "personal car" is Ford's ball-joint suspension and a sturdy,

rigid X member frame with boxed side rails. They combine to give the T-Bird a comfortable, but firm and sports car-type ride on any surface. The test crew found the ride so much like the quick-reacting European sports cars, that the power steering (with reduced steering ratio) still seemed slow. To Americans with sports car driving experience, the car will seem to react to the wheel slowly. For those used to conventional steering, the response will seem quite rapid. It will require some getting-to-know-you driving for both groups. Those with Ford power steering on their previous family cars, will adapt most rapidly to it. The remaining groups may take all of 15 or 20 minutes to "get the hang of that steering." Pulled hard over, the T-Bird does strange things for an American car; it arcs in its own tracks. For drivers who have never handled a car with a tight turning radius, the experience will be new—and exciting. With a tight, say, 2.75 or 3 turns lock-to-lock conventional steering, the Thunderbird would be one of the most directly maneuverable cars available—from either side of the Atlantic. One drawback to this theory, however, is the Thunderbird's weight. Only 175 inches bumper to bumper, the T-Bird is well constructed, weighs as much, curbside, as the Ford club coupe. Our test cars averaged 3225 pounds, and with 52% of that on the front wheels, a tight, direct steering would be aimed directly at male drivers.

T-Bird features the 1955 Ford automatic transmission (or is available with conventional and/or overdrive) which starts off in Drive-low, instead of the 1954 Drive-intermediate. The automatic shifts, under full throttle, come in at an average of 30 mph and 60 mph. The Fordomatic transmission, however, can practically be shifted at will. With a slow, rolling start, one can be in Drive-direct by 20 mph. The more throttle, the more each gear will wind.

In Fordomatic Drive Range, when the throttle is fully depressed, there is a momentary lag, a split-second hesitation

while the car hunches its shoulders for the job ahead. First driver reaction for that split-second is "it's got no pick up." Just about the time that thought is formed, something catches and the Thunderbird begins to move—and move. Although it won't out-drag some of the expensive foreign iron, the Thunderbird accelerates quite rapidly, clambers up to 60 mph in 10.75 seconds, stays strong on acceleration all the way up to a true 80 mph, where it begins to flatten out slightly. By getting to 30 mph in 4.30 seconds, the Thunderbird appears to be a real stoplight menace and it's going to take a lot more inches for the production hot rods to catch it.

Passing the 100 mph mark, the Thunderbird holds strong and true to the road, the speedo needle continues to climb steadily. Maximum speed for the Thunderbird, with automatic transmission, was 118 mph with the Fordomatic 3.31:1 gear ratio. Overdrive-equipped cars will hit 120 plus.

The Thunderbird, throughout the two testing periods, turned in average gasoline mileages of 15 mpg for city driving, 17.5 mpg for steady highway cruising.

One design item which puzzled the MOTOR *Life* test staff was the dual exhaust setup.

While Ford engineers have evidently "sold" the advantages of the dual exhaust system, the stylists have somewhat negated the engineering effort by placing a series of bends in the exhaust lines, ending up with two 90 degree turns which bring the exhaust tips out through the high-placed bumper guards. It would require a complicated analysis to illustrate the harmful effect of this move but it's general knowledge that exhaust lines should be as straight as a driveshaft. Considering chassis design, this isn't always possible—but it should be heavily considered at all times.

Summed up, the Thunderbird combines all of the best boulevard sports car qualities with a reasonable price, good dependability and what should be an excellent resale. Operating costs should be comparable to the everyday passenger car and the performance is far superior. It is well designed, has a rigid steel body, excellent handling and ride characteristics plus all of the comforts and conveniences Americans have come to expect in an automobile. Only the die-hard sports car enthusiasts (those who drive in the rain without putting the top up) will look askance at the windows and power equipment. But they're a hardy lot—still waiting for the return of the Jordan Playboy.

Early Indian tribes believed that the Thunderbird caused lightning by opening and closing its eyes, thunder by flapping its wings. Its high-performance automotive namesake will undoubtedly cause just as much disturbance—among automobile enthusiasts and those who like to drive for the pure fun of it. ●

Seventh heaven on wheels—

the Ford THUNDERBIRD

Wherever—whenever—your Thunderbird appears in public, the effect is electric. All eyes turn to its long, low, graceful beauty. All hearts say "That's for me!"

And if they only knew the full story! If they could spend but half an hour in *your* seat. If they could listen to the dual-throated harmony of its tuned mufflers and twin exhausts. If they could feel the steepest hills melt before the might of the 198-h.p. Thunderbird Special V-8. If they could see the tachometer needle wind up, as the four-barrel carburetor and 8.5 to 1 compression ratio convert gasoline into road-ruling Trigger-Torque "Go"!

Then they could sample a portion of your pride in *your* personal car. But you could show them more!

You could show them the way it takes the corners as if magnetized to the road. You could let them feel the lightning "take-off" with new Speed-Trigger Fordomatic Drive.

You could show them how quickly the convertible top whisks into place—how easily the solid top lifts on and off—the all-steel body—the ample trunk space—the rich interiors—the telescoping steering wheel —the 4-way power seat.

Should your Thunderbird have the optional power assists, they could note the convenience of

power steering, power brakes and power window lifts.

You could show them this and more—how even routine driving becomes thrilling entertainment.

Yes, we're day-dreaming for you. But why not put yourself in the driver's seat and make this dream come true? The man to see is your Ford Dealer.

An exciting original by FORD

MARCH-APRIL 1955

The lines of the Thunderbird are simple but striking, marred only by the exterior mounting of the spare wheel and the unhappy porthole

The Autocar ROAD TESTS

No. 1588

FORD THUNDERBIRD

THERE has been considerable speculation in Europe about the U.S. Ford Thunderbird since its introduction at the Paris Show in October, 1954. Not since the late 'twenties has a major American manufacturer attempted production of a really high performance sports touring car. To *The Autocar* has fallen the pleasure of completing the first full Road Test to be made on this side of the Atlantic, and it may be said at once that the task was unusually absorbing.

The car was provided by the British concessionaires, Lincoln Cars, Ltd., Great West Road, Brentford, Middlesex, who raised British interest in the model above the merely academic by stating that models are available for sterling purchase.

Every car tester asks himself first just what the model is supposed to be, and for what type of market it is intended to cater. The Ford answer is that the Thunderbird is a fast touring car combining speed with luxury; that it is not a sports or sports-racing car. But when familiarity with the model grows one cannot help feeling that the two-seat-tourer description is a tongue-in-cheek line on the part of the manufacturer. For the

Thunderbird will reach a true 100 m.p.h. in less than 32 seconds with plenty still in hand; the steering is positive, and on the indifferently surfaced roads of France (where much of the testing took place) it will cruise at 90-plus without road adhesion being reduced to a dangerous or unpleasant degree.

The car tested was provided with many extras that push up the cost price substantially. The detachable hardtop is included in the basic price of £1,690 (making £2,536 7s with purchase tax), but when all extras are included the basic price becomes £2,075 (making £3,115 1s). The extras include Fordomatic transmission, power brakes, a soft hood for use when the hardtop is left in the garage, a nine-valve radio (costing £75 with tax), heater, windscreen washer, and so on, all of which were fitted to the car described here.

The specification of the car is worth examination before comfort and performance are described in any detail, for the American approach to the high performance two-seater is different from that adopted in Europe. The engine is characteristically American, being a relatively low-revving 5,113 c.c.

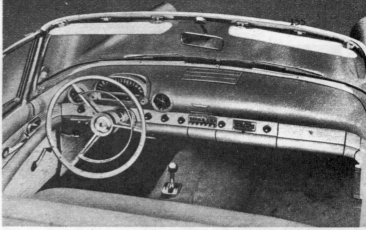

(312 cu in) capacity unit with overhead valves operated by push-rods. Maximum b.h.p. is 225 at 4,600 r.p.m., and maximum torque 324 lb ft at 2,600 r.p.m. When orthodox transmission with overdrive is fitted, instead of the automatic, power output is 215 b.h.p. and torque 317 lb ft. The compression ratio on the car tested was 9 to 1, while the manual transmission model has 8.4 to 1. Overall weight is about 31 cwt ready for the road, but although this seems heavy to Europeans for a two-seater, the b.h.p. per ton laden with occupants is an exciting 132—only nominally short of the most powerful comparable British sports two-seater coupé. The extra weight compared with European counterparts results in some degree from the luxuries with which this car is equipped and which are not always found on the out-and-out sports car.

Despite the manufacturer's decision to call the car, in effect, a boulevard model, the performance is such as to clamour for description, and in this connection the automatic transmission must be closely related to the acceleration. The Fordomatic has three ratios, gear-change speeds depending largely upon throttle opening. When the throttle pedal is fully depressed from a standing start, the transmission changes from first to second at 35 m.p.h., and from second to top at 62 m.p.h. Below about 55 m.p.h. full depression of the pedal results in a "kick down" in to the middle ratio. Coupled with this effect is the operation of the four-choke carburettor. A resistance is felt when the pedal is depressed through half its range. Until this occurs only two chokes are in operation, but beyond it the other two chokes begin to operate. Thus, when putting the pedal flat down at, say, 40 m.p.h., middle gear is engaged at the same moment as the two extra chokes—or carburettors, in effect—come into operation. The results would be gratifying to the most *blasé* of testers. When overtaking, this mechanism is seen at its best, and although European drivers expect cars of similar potential speed to be capable of much more than 62 m.p.h. in the indirect gears, the power output of the Thunderbird engine is such that the acceleration on top from 62 upwards is very good indeed, as is shown by the acceleration data.

The car is deceptive. It was tested in weather that varied from the ideal to snow and ice, and in all but the most slippery conditions it achieved average speeds that surprised even the driver. The automatic transmission put it at a disadvantage on really slippery surfaces, as the slip at low r.p.m. might deceive a driver into thinking that the rear wheels are spinning, when, in fact, the rise in r.p.m. results only from the drive being taken up gently in the automatic mechanism. If the car does slide on any surface it is immediately controllable, partly because the steering has only four turns from lock to lock which, coupled with the excellent lock itself, is a modest figure. On main road corners there is no question of winding the steering, and quick corrections can be made without moving the hands on the wheel. The degree of understeer is slight and there is no undue runout on fast corners.

Initially, the suspension feels soft for a car of such high potential performance, for at low speeds on poor surfaces the comfort is more characteristic of the family saloon than the high speed two-seater. However, roll is limited, and as the speed rises the initial softness gives way to appropriately firm springing. True, the suspension—and handling as a whole—is not up to the highest standards of European *gran turismo* machinery, but the compromise between the boulevard and real sports car has a strong bias in the latter's favour.

Some idea of its capabilities was provided on runs between

The facia is well laid out, although the moulding at its base is carried across the doors to little purpose. A fire extinguisher is mounted on the extreme right of the compartment, and the automatic mechanism for adjusting the fore-and-aft and vertical setting of the bench seat is controlled from two switches in the driver's door

Le Touquet, in France, and Ostend, in Belgium. On the route through Boulogne, Calais and Dunkirk the roads have many straights but are rather narrow and rarely smooth; yet on most open stretches the Thunderbird was safely held between a true 90 and 100 m.p.h. At this speed in the conditions described the car was bumpy, but not to the extent of real passenger discomfort, and adhesion remained satisfactory. Again, on a run at a bad time of day from the river, in central London, to Ferryfield, on the Kent south coast, driver and passenger were more than a little surprised at an overall time of little over 1½ hours, in spite of one long hold up for road works in London, and road surfaces often lightly covered with melting snow. The engine is unobtrusive until about 100 m.p.h. is reached on the speedometer, which embodies no more than the accepted built-in optimism as our recorded figures on page 157 indicate.

Europeans (and some Americans, too) have mixed feelings about the use of automatic transmission on this type of car, but before plumping for a manual change with overdrive, let the Fordomatic be more carefully considered. When high average speeds are not required, the car accelerates well with gentle use of the throttle, covering the ground in a restful, effortless fashion, the transmission being seen at its best. But when the driver really wants to hustle, the automatic box is surprisingly co-operative. On modern dual carriageways overtaking is in any case usually accomplished in top gear; on British roads at anything from a crawl upwards. At, say, 40-50 m.p.h. when waiting for a clear stretch in which to overtake, the driver with manual transmission will frequently be changing up and down, waiting his chance, or trailing the other vehicle in the lowest gear appropriate to the speed. But with the Fordomatic he remains in top and, at the moment a short, clear stretch is sighted, a jab of the throttle instantly produces middle gear and the extra carburettor chokes with delightful results. Having in mind engine size and performance the m.p.g. is not unreasonable, 16 being obtained under quite hard driving conditions.

One objection to some automatic transmissions is that they may change down when slowing into corners with results that can be particularly unwelcome on slippery surfaces. Suffice it to say of the Fordomatic tested that unless the change was induced by the driver it occurred at very low speeds and was extremely smooth—to the point of being virtually imperceptible. No driver was embarrassed by it while it was in the hands of this journal.

On the subject of brakes we cannot be complimentary to the Thunderbird. In fact, all too often are brakes and

A soft hood is available as an optional extra for erection when the hardtop is left in the garage. It is well tailored, and has a wide rear window, but it takes a very long time—and two people—to put up

Wide doors make entry reasonably easy for a car of such low build. The steering wheel spokes are dished so that they act as a shock absorber for the driver's chest in the event of an accident

A big air cleaner is fitted above the four-choke carburettor. In this view the distributor is to the left, and the oil filler to the right. Beyond this is seen the plastic container for the windscreen washer. The battery is accessible on the far side of the engine, and, close to the camera, are the equally accessible dipsticks for transmission and engine oil levels

FORD THUNDERBIRD . . .

brake fade the subject of criticism on high-performance cars. During the test their efficiency varied appreciably, but the overall impression was of good response to very light pedal pressure at low speeds (indeed, the wheels could be locked with moderate pedal pressure) and a sharp fall off in efficiency coupled with grab at very high speeds. At speeds close to the formidable maximum the brakes had to be used with caution,

lines. But these are small criticisms of an otherwise most attractive conception. The bonnet (or hood to American readers) hinges at its forward edge and, sensibly, flexible dipsticks are provided for the engine and transmission oils so that the handles are conveniently placed. The luggage locker lid must be opened with a key, after movement of a lever swings the spare wheel slightly backwards to give clearance. The spare wheel must also be moved to provide access to the central tank filler. The filler is covered with a hinged flap in which there is a protruding bolt just waiting to scratch the hand of anyone opening the cap.

Considerable attention is paid to seating position; movement of the seat backwards and forwards, and up and down, was effected by electric motors operated by two switches in the driver's door. The steering column is adjustable for reach, and the inwardly dished three spokes protrude towards the driver to provide a shock absorbing effect in the event of an accident, helping to reduce to a minimum any impact of the driver's chest against the column. The heavily-swept-round windscreen provides good visibility, although there is some distortion at the sides and the padded visors intrude at the top.

The bulge on the bonnet is a fresh air intake. Additional ventilators are fitted on the sides, and fog and spot lamps are incorporated in the front bumper assembly

Movement of a lever immediately in front of the spare wheel casing permits the wheel to move rearwards to enable the luggage locker lid to be opened. When the boot lid is closed, a small cover gives access to the fuel filler cap. Luggage space is substantial, but of a shape that gives soft bags an advantage over orthodox suitcases. The rear lights are surrounded by large reflectors

as initial application frequently resulted in a sharp pull to one side or the other. From high speeds the car needed plenty of room in which to stop. On the relatively clear roads of the Continent, the brakes caused little trouble, and in England icy roads saved them for much of the time.

The appearance of the car attracted attention wherever it was parked; it is dramatic to look at as well as to drive. In the current U.S. sports fashion the spare wheel is mounted in a visible container at the rear. A feature of the pre-war European sports coupés, such a mounting now seems an anachronism to our eyes. The extent to which the otherwise attractive lines are marred may be judged by removing the spare wheel and taking another look at the car. The porthole shape of the useful small windows in the hardtop is also out of accord with the general

A feature of all Fords is the suction operated windscreen wiper. It is one which has little appeal to many motorists and in the case of this Thunderbird it amounted to a definite fault. Every time the driver accelerated to pass another vehicle the wiper stopped and in wet weather the screen became obscured and overtaking was made hazardous or impossible. Further, the wipers leave an awkwardly placed unwiped wedge in the centre of the screen that obscures visibility of the far wing. This is accentuated by the positioning of the steering wheel close to the side of the car. In a wide two-seater of this type most drivers would, in in any case, prefer the wheel to be farther inboard to provide more room for the outer elbow. Reflections from the decking behind the seat tend at night to give the illusion that one is being followed.

Controls are well arranged and clearly labelled. The transmission lever is nearly central, and the speedometer directly in front of the driver. The latter is not very easy to read, partly because it is graduated up to an impressive 150 m.p.h. The powerful heater with two-speed fan provides warm fresh air, recirculation, or cold air ventilation, which can be directed in any proportion to the interior or the screen at easily controlled temperature.

Among the many lavish items of equipment is an exceptionally fine radio with nine valves. Stations can be chosen by button, or by touching either of two bars at which the set will seek automatically, stopping perfectly tuned on any station it comes across until a bar is touched again. One bar gives greater selectivity than the other, and the set is such that Moscow was received with faultless clarity and volume after midnight, and Italy similarly before dawn. There was no fading whatsoever even under bridges.

A hard but shock-absorbent roll below the facia is carried round and back across the doors at elbow level. If this roll served as an armrest it would be a better feature; as it is, it makes it more difficult to operate the window winder.

The Thunderbird has arrived as a pleasant surprise, there being a great deal to be said for the clever compromise between comfort and very high performance indeed.

FORD THUNDERBIRD

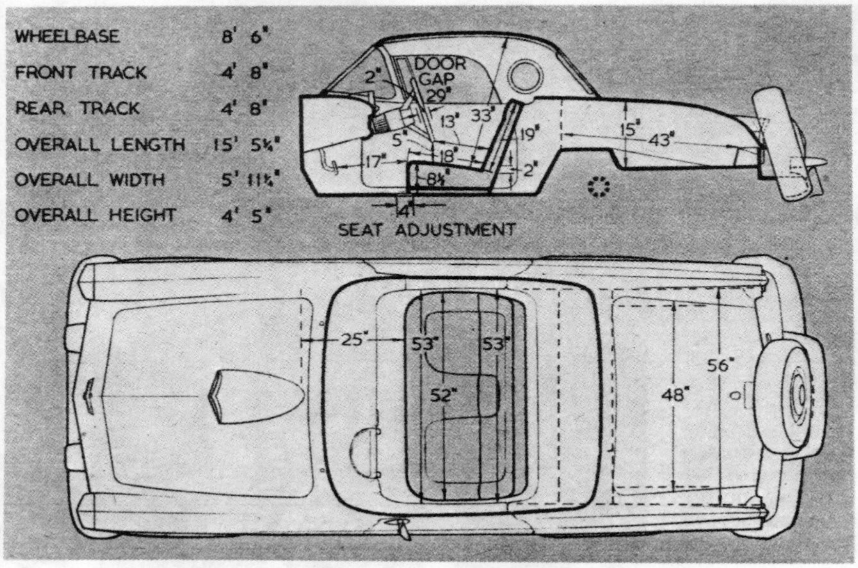
WHEELBASE 8' 6"
FRONT TRACK 4' 8"
REAR TRACK 4' 8"
OVERALL LENGTH 15' 5¼"
OVERALL WIDTH 5' 11¼"
OVERALL HEIGHT 4' 5"
DOOR GAP 29"
2"
13"
33"
5"
17"
18"
19"
8½"
2"
15"
43"
4"
SEAT ADJUSTMENT
25"
53"
53"
52"
48"
56"

Measurements in these ¼in to 1ft scale body diagrams are taken with the driving seat in the central position of fore and aft adjustment and with the seat cushions uncompressed

DATA

PRICE (basic), with two-seater body, **£1,690.**
British purchase tax, **£846 7s.**
Total (in Great Britain), **£2,536 7s.**
Extras: Radio **£75.** Heater **£56 5s.** Fordomatic transmission, **£144.**
Total British price as tested, **£3,115 1s.**

ENGINE: Capacity: 5,113 c.c. (312 cu in).
Number of cylinders: 8.
Bore and stroke: 96.52 × 87.37 mm (3.8 × 3.44in).
Valve gear: o.h.v. pushrods.
Compression ratio: 9 to 1.
B.H.P.: 225 at 4,600 r.p.m. (B.H.P. per ton laden 132.3).
Torque: 324 lb ft at 2,600 r.p.m.
M.P.H. per 1,000 r.p.m. on top gear, 25.

WEIGHT (with 5 gals fuel): 31 cwt (3,472 lb).
Weight distribution (per cent): F, 50; R, 50.
Laden as tested: 34 cwt (3,808 lb).
Lb per c.c. (laden): 1.3.

BRAKES: Type, leading and trailing shoes.
Method of operation: Hydraulic.
Drum dimensions: F, 11in diameter; 1¾in and 2¼in wide.
R, 11in diameter; 1¾in wide.
Lining area: F, 91 sq in. R, 79 sq in (100 sq in per ton laden).

TYRES: 6.70—15in.
Pressures (lb per sq in): F, 24; R, 24 (normal). F, 30; R, 30 (for fast driving).

TANK CAPACITY: 13.6 Imperial gallons.
Oil sump, 8 pints.
Cooling system, 32 pints (plus 2 pints if heater is fitted).

TURNING CIRCLE: 36ft (L and R).
Steering wheel turns (lock to lock): 4.

DIMENSIONS: Wheelbase: 8ft 6in.
Track: F, 4ft 8in; R, 4ft 8in.
Length (overall): 15ft 5¼in.
Height: 4ft 4½in.
Width: 5ft 10½in.
Ground clearance: 5.9in.

ELECTRICAL SYSTEM: 12-volt; 55 ampère-hour battery.
Head lights: Double dip; 50-40 watt bulbs.

SUSPENSION: Front, independent. Rear, semi-elliptic.

PERFORMANCE

ACCELERATION: from constant speeds. Speed Range, *Gear Ratios and Time in sec.

M.P.H.	Dr. range
10—30	2.7
20—40	3.4
30—50	4.0
40—60	5.1
50—70	6.6
60—80	8.3

From rest through gears to:

M.P.H.	sec.
30	3.4
50	7.4
60	10.2
70	14.0
80	18.5
90	23.9
100	31.8

*Gear ratios 3.31; 4.86; and 7.94 to 1.
Standing quarter mile, 17.5 sec.

SPEEDS ON GEARS:

Gear		M.P.H. (max.)	K.P.H. (max.)
Top	(mean)	113	181.8
	(best)	116	186.7
2nd		62	99.8
1st		35	56.3

TRACTIVE RESISTANCE: 40 lb per ton at 10 M.P.H.

TRACTIVE EFFORT:

	Pull (lb per ton)	Equivalent Gradient
Top	337	1 in 6.6
Second	600	1 in 3.6

BRAKES:

Efficiency	Pedal Pressure (lb)
62 per cent	25
75 per cent	40

FUEL CONSUMPTION:
16.5 m.p.g. overall for 714 miles (26.5 litres per 100 km).
Approximate normal range 15-18 m.p.g. (24-29 litres per 100 km).
Fuel, first grade.

WEATHER: Dry, light wind.
Air temperature: 32 deg F.
Acceleration figures are the means of several runs in opposite directions.
Tractive effort and resistance obtained by Tapley meter.

SPEEDOMETER CORRECTION: M.P.H.

Car speedometer	10	20	30	40	50	60	70	80	90	100	110	121
True speed	8	18	28	38	46	56	64	75	85	96	105	116

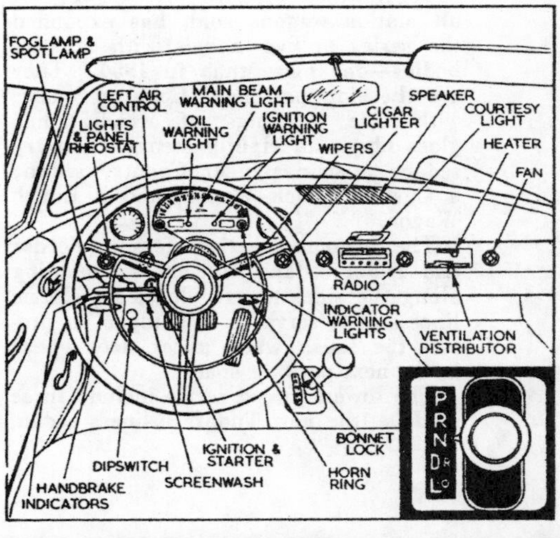
FOGLAMP & SPOTLAMP
LEFT AIR CONTROL
MAIN BEAM WARNING LIGHT
SPEAKER
COURTESY LIGHT
LIGHTS & PANEL RHEOSTAT
OIL WARNING LIGHT
IGNITION WARNING LIGHT
WIPERS
CIGAR LIGHTER
HEATER
FAN
RADIO
INDICATOR WARNING LIGHTS
VENTILATION DISTRIBUTOR
BONNET LOCK
HORN RING
IGNITION & STARTER
SCREENWASH
DIPSWITCH
HANDBRAKE
INDICATORS
P R N D L

The 1955 Ford

The Fairlane Crown Victoria has a chrome strip running across the top of the car. The model is also available with a transparent roof over the driver's compartment.

FORD introduced an entirely new line—the high-styled Fairlane series —as the leader of its four lines of passenger cars for 1955.

Included in the new Fairlane series, named after the home of the late Henry Ford, is a completely new styling idea— the Crown Victoria. The first Ford sedan under five feet in overall height, the Crown Victoria has an arch of chrome over the top like a tiara. It is also available with a transparent plastic roof over the driver's compartment.

The line also includes the Sunliner convertible, the Victoria, the four-door Town sedan and the two-door Club sedan.

Ford, which produces 47 per cent of all station wagons sold, has expanded the series to five models with all-steel bodies—one more than in 1954. They are the eight-passenger Country Squire, with side moldings of wood-grained glass fibre; an eight-passenger Country sedan; a six-passenger Country sedan; a Custom Ranch Wagon, and a Ranch Wagon.

The Customline series offers the Fordor and Tudor sedans with chrome molding along the sides to provide clean, classic lines and to serve as a 'bumper' to protect the finish when a car door opens in the next parking space.

The lowest priced series include three models—the new Tudor Business sedan,

the Tudor sedan and the Fordor sedan.

The Thunderbird, Ford's 'personal car,' gave an advance hint of the company's styling trend when it was unveiled earlier. Measuring just 4 feet, 4.2 inches high in the hardtop model, the Thunderbird will accommodate three people, with rear compartment space for their luggage. It was designed for a combination of high performance with the comfort, convenience and safety of a conventional car. The adjustable steering wheel slides in or out three inches and can be locked in the position the driver prefers. A power seat is standard equipment.

Ford, which offered the first V-8 engine in the low-price field in 1932, has now introduced three new engines: a high compression Y-block V-8 engine of 272 cubic inch displacement and a 8.5 to 1 compression ratio; a powerful Y-block V-engine of 272 cubic inch displacement and a 7.6 to 1 compression ratio, and an improved six-cylinder I-block engine of 223 cubic inch displacement and a 7.5 to 1 compression ratio.

Dual exhausts, which provide extra power, are standard on all Fairlane V-8 and station wagon models.

The longer, lower bodies of the new Fords, with the wraparound windshield, is shown here in the Fairlane four-door sedan. Both the Y-block V-8 and the I-block Six cylinder engines are offered by the company.

A new, lower silhouette with modern styling inspired by the 'Thunderbird' distinguishes the four lines of passenger cars this year

Auto Review

Ford's new 'personal' car is the all-steel Thunderbird with a telescopic steering column. A semi-sports car, it is available either as a hardtop or a convertible.

Above: Ford's latest car is the Fairlane Crown Victoria, a more lavishly-styled model than others in the Ford range. It has an arch of chromium running right over the top of the car.

Different appearance and more power from the V8 and sixes head American Ford improvements this year.

AMERICAN Ford have boosted the horsepower of their overhead valve V-8, introduced last year, from 130 b.h.p. to 162 b.h.p.

No U.S. Fords will be available in Australia.

A new line of cars, called the Fairlane (after Henry Ford's home) has a higher powered version still of the 4.4 litre V-8.

It develops 182 b.h.p., has a compression ratio of 8.5 to 1 instead of 7.6 to 1, a four barrel carburettor and dual exhausts.

This new engine is supplied only on Fairlanes equipped with "Fordomatic" automatic transmission.

But any of the sixteen different models in the Ford range can be equipped either with the 162 b h.p. V-8 or the 120 b.h.p. straight six.

The six has overhead valves, a displacement of 3.7 litres and a 7.5 to 1 compression.

Another improvement is to the automatic transmission. Faster acceleration from rest is available by pressing the accelerator to the floor. This cuts in "low" range.

In last year's models the driver had to engage the "low" range of the transmission by hand if he wanted this extra acceleration.

Ford's "Thunderbird," a low-slung two-seater semi-sports car put into production last year, has set the styling and frontal appearance for the rest of the 1955 models.

The "Fairlane" series has more luxurious trim and finish than the standard Fords. One model, the Crown Victoria, has an arch of chromium plating right over the car.

U.S. FORDS for 1955

All Mercurys are lower, wider and longer. This rear view of the new Montclair series (left) shows the lower silhouette. Chrome is extensively used on this series.

February 1955

It has a windscreen which curves right around the corners where the pillars were placed in older models. The pillars are now vertical, thus giving the driver a clearer view of the road.

The Fairlane is Ford's first car outside the Thunderbird to be less than five feet in overall height.

The Thunderbird has a 193 b.h.p. V-8 engine and a standard three-speed transmission. Automatic drive is optional, and with it goes a 198 b.h.p. engine, gained by raising the compression from 8 to 8.5 to 1.

An adjustable steering column and power-operated seat adjustment are standard. Power steering, power window lifts and power brakes are optional.

Wind-up windows, a detachable hard top and a fold-down convertible top are standard equipment.

Ford are also offering air-conditioning (both heating and cooling) equipment as optional on all models. The equipment is fitted in the engine compartment. Some early types of air conditioning equipment took up space in the boot.

All Ford's power equipment—seat adjustment, window lifts, breaking, transmission and steering—is optional right through the range.

Slight modifications have been made to the ball-joint front suspension, introduced last year, and brake lining area has been increased on all models.

Tubeless tyres are standard on some models and optional on others.

MERCURY

Engine improvements and higher outputs have been extended to the Mercury range as well.

A new series of cars—the Mercury Montclair—has an 8.5 to 1 V-8 engine giving 198 b.h.p. at 4,400 r.p.m. Torque is 286 lb./ft.

The engines in other Mercurys have a 7.6 to 1 compression and develop 188 b.h.p. and 274 lb./ft.

All have a capacity of 4.8 litres.

Improvements have been made to the four-barrel carburettor, the fuel pump is bigger and placed in the air stream, the combustion chamber has been redesigned and new, no-gasket conical spark plugs are used.

Dual exhausts are standard on Montclair models and optional on the others.

The automatic transmission has been improved.

Wheelbase on all 10 models has been lengthened to 9'11", and width and length have been increased 2". All models are lower, some as much as 2½".

Brake lining area has been increased from 159 to 191 sq. in.

Other features are tubeless tyres as standard, an automatic chassis lubrication system as optional, and many new choices of colours and upholstery.

The same list of power equipment available for Fords is available for Mercurys.

The Thunderbird (right) is now in steady production, and even though sales will be limited, it is a "prestige" car, valuable in that it shows buyers that U.S. factories can match imported efforts and translate them into automatic-transmission, boulevarde-ride style cars accepted as American "personal" automobiles.

Mercury's new Montclair (below) has a wrap around windshield and a 198 horsepower V-8 engine. Note the hoods over the headlights.

testing FORD'S "Personal" Car

The T-Bird Shows its Claws

Power accessories fill all available space.

WITH ALL the interest in Ford's new Thunderbird "personal car", the performance claims of overly enthusiastic salesmen can perhaps be excused. In a quick survey of 5 salesrooms we casually asked about the top speed of the T-Bird—and got replies varying from 125 to 150 mph! But it is a little more difficult to justify the published figures given out in purported road tests on this car, which range from 115 to 130 mph.

Admittedly it isn't the easiest thing to get an accurate timed top speed run on a car—there have been times when we've had to skip this test ourselves. But in this case, our approach to the performance testing phase of the Thunderbird was to be as thorough and complete in our evaluation as was humanly possible.

The first step in any road test is to obtain a suitable car. Of course we could buy one—but that's the easy way. Quite by chance we found an enthusiastic R & T reader who not only had a T-Bird with 2500 miles on it, but also was ready and anxious to let us test the car. The man was Bob Alley of Arcadia, California, who also owns a Jaguar and a Porsche and is a true enthusiast without prejudice or bias.

The second step is to insure that the car to be tested is in top condition and capable of giving a typical performance, truly representative of the car in question. In this case the factory bent over backward and the car spent four hours in the famous Clay Smith shop from which come the Mexican race-winning Lincolns.

Having, by now, a well-tuned car, the

photographs by Rolofson

next step was to obtain the services of a top driver. In this case we chose Jack Mc-Afee, who did most of the driving during the performance checks. Bill Corey, who writes our Tune Up Clinic and who is notoriously addicted to supercharged Jaguars also drove the car for a short while, along with the Editor.

The car itself was one of the early deliveries, fully equipped with Fordomatic transmission, heater, power steering, power brakes, power seat, power windows and the folding cluth top. It cost its owner just under $4000, delivered, but cars can be purchased without the power gadgets for $2695 (plus freight, tax and license). With a full tank of gas, it weighed 3240 lbs. The driver, observor and test equipment added 380 lbs, for a total test weight of 3620 lbs. All tests were run at this weight (minus 3 or 4 gallons used), with top in place and windows closed. Tire pressure was 30 psi, as recommended for high speed work.

The high speed runs began after a drive of 140 miles, with the outside temperature at 40° F, altitude zero. There was a light breeze and the two best timed runs in opposite directions recorded 107.9 and 112.3 mph respectively. The car would "peak out" in about 1½ miles and the respective tachometer readings were 4500 against and 4600 rpm with the wind. During the best one-way run the speedometer needle indicated and held 125/126 mph for ½ mile before entering the surveyed time trap. Since this car was equipped with the higher com-

Although the Thunderbird lines are smooth wind resistance proved to be rather high.

pression, 198 bhp engine and a 3.31 axle ratio, it appears quite unlikely that any other combination of gear ratio or transmission will produce more than 112 mph. The engine peaks at 4400 rpm and the 3.31 axle is as near ideal for best possible top speed on this car as it is possible to achieve. Overdrive equipment, with a 2.74 overall ratio would give only 3850 rpm at 112 mph and the engine would not be capable of pulling the car that fast, at 550 rpm below its peak power speed. Reports of 128/130 mph in overdrive can therefore be relegated to the category of speedometer readings, downhill.

Few cars tested by us, have been given

ROAD & TRACK ROAD TEST NO. A-3-55
FORD THUNDERBIRD

SPECIFICATIONS

List price	$2695
Wheelbase	102 in.
Tread	56 in.
Tire size	6.70-15
Curb weight	3240 lbs
distribution	52/48
Test weight	3620 lbs
Engine	V-8
Valves	pohv
Bore & stroke	3.75 x 3.30
Displacement	292 cu in. (4788 cc)
Compression ratio	8.50
Horsepower	198
peaking speed	4400
equivalent mph	106
Torque, ft/lbs	286
peaking speed	2500
equivalent mph	60.5
Mph per 1000 rpm	24.2
Mph at 2500 fpm	110

Gear ratios (overall)

3rd	3.31
2nd	4.87
1st	7.94
1st + converter	16.7
R & T perf. factor	66.8

PERFORMANCE

Top speed (avg)	110.1
best run	112.3
Max speeds in gears—	
2nd (5000)	82
1st (5000)	50
Shift points from—	
2nd (4500)	74
1st (4500)	45
Mileage	15/18 mpg

ACCELERATION

0-30 mph	3.7 secs
0-40 mph	5.6 secs
0-50 mph	7.6 secs
0-60 mph	9.5 secs
0-70 mph	13.9 secs
0-80 mph	17.8 secs
0-90 mph	23.0 secs
Standing ¼ mile—	
average	17.1 secs
best	16.9 secs

TAPLEY READINGS

Gear	Lbs/ton	Mph	Grade
1st	600	at 30	33%
2nd	430	at 37	22%
3rd	340	at 54	17%
Total drag at 60 mph, 190 lbs			

SPEEDO ERROR

Indicated	Actual
10	9.8
20	17.5
30	26.2
40	35.6
50	43.9
60	52.4
70	62.1
80	71.9
90	80.8
100	90.0

FORD THUNDERBIRD (Fordomatic) acceleration through the gears
USING "FORCED" SHIFTS
STARTING IN "DRIVE" — — — —

ROAD and TRACK

such lengthy testing for acceleration times. This came about for two reasons: 1) to secure accurate results which, when averaged, could be duplicated by any similar car and 2) the necessity of utilizing to best advantage certain peculiarities of the automatic transmission.

The Fordomatic unit has 3 speeds forward, coupled to a torque converter which becomes an efficient fluid coupling at high speed. Normally we test automatic transmissions in "Drive" and also attempt to get better times by various techniques. With this transmission it is possible to overrule the normal functioning in such a way as to reduce the zero to 60 mph acceleration time by over 1.5 seconds. Here's how it's done. Rev the engine at 2000 rpm with selector in neutral. Pull the lever quickly into Low range and hit the throttle when the tires begin to churn. There is a one or two second lag between lever movement and car movement and too much throttle gives excessive wheelspin with a tendency for the rear end to move sideways (to the right). Once underway, with just the right amount of tire chirp, the throttle is opened wide. An engine speed of 4500 rpm proved to be the optimum shift point and at this point the lever is moved to Drive, still maintaining full throttle. The transmission shifts from first to second gear at this time, speed about 45 mph. Left in Drive it will shift to high at about 58 mph, at only 3800 rpm. To avoid this, the lever is quickly moved back to Low range, the speed being now around 50/55 mph, this forces the Fordo-

matic to stay in second gear—forever, if desired. However at 4500 in second (lever in low range) equivalent to 74 mph (82 indicated) the lever is again snapped into Drive. This effects a shift to third (high) gear. At no time during this maneuver is the throttle released. Shifts are almost instantaneous and reasonably smooth. Except for the start, the process does not seem abusive in any way and as a matter of fact we found the high revving start in neutral unnecessary. Holding the left foot on the brake, with the lever in Low gave equal times with less strain on the drive train. Our usual acceleration graph shows the results of using the gears to best advantage ("forced" shifts) as compared to using drive range only. A tabulation also shows the comparison in acceleration times.

Speed-Mph	Drive range	"Forced" shifts
0-30	3.9 secs	3.7 secs
0-40	6.1 secs	5.6 secs
0-50	8.2 secs	7.6 secs
0-60	11.1 secs	9.5 secs
0-70	14.6 secs	13.9 secs
0-80	18.5 secs	17.8 secs
0-90	24.5 secs	23.0 secs
ss ¼	17.6 secs	16.9 secs

The Tapley readings in each gear are given in the data panel, along with something new—the equivalent % grade which can be climbed at a steady speed in each gear.

General impressions formed regarding the T-Bird are most favorable. The Ford Motor Co. refrains from calling this car a sports car, but we think this policy is being overly cautious. Even the die-hard sports car fan will admit that the natural evolution of the "type" has gone somewhat beyond the purist's definition of "a car suitable for both every-day and competition driving." Today's sports cars can readily be divided into 3 categories, 1) all-out competition, 2) dual-purpose, and 3) touring-sports types. The Thunderbird can and will be entered in sports car competitions, but even in stripped and modified form it hasn't much of a chance in the highly competitive class C category (3 to 5 litres). The Thunderbird is a touring-sports car, designed ot give sports car qualities up to a point, combined with enough comfort to satisfy the most delicate of constitutions. It is an extremely practical machine for personal transport over any distance in any kind of weather.

The cockpit is exceptionally roomy and comfortable, will even accommodate three

adults occasionally—a 2/3 seater. The controls are well placed with no peculiarities which require practice or accommodation. The adjustable steering column, with an in or out movement of 3″ is an excellent feature and the low set steering wheel is well placed for a driver of average height. The riding qualities are really excellent and the equal of any sports car we've ever driven.

Our test car had the optional power steering (3.6 turns lock to lock) a feature which we felt to be completely unnecessary, though not objectionable. There is a moderate degree of understeer, somewhat difficult to evaluate because of the power steering. Owners who wish to reduce the understeer can use front tire pressures as high as 30/32 psi, and rear tires at 24 psi. We did not have the opportunity of making this experiment but cars equipped with non-power steering might be cornered with less effort by introducing the above tire pressure changes. Jack McAfee reported that the car felt very safe and stable during the timed speed runs.

Wind noise, at high speeds is rather obtrusive, and a strange hum sets in at over 70 mph which appears to emanate from the carburetor air scoop. The owner reports that the interior remains dry in the heaviest rainstorm but the edges of the cloth top lift slightly, at speed, at a point midway along the top of each side window. The 292 cubic inch Mercury engine is smooth and quiet at all times, but economy during highway cruising at 65/70 mph (indicated) was a little lower than might be expected (15.0 mpg). The best economy figure we've heard is 18 mpg under similar conditions on an overdrive model.

We were disappointed with the excessive speedometer optimism found on the test car, a feature which appears to be so typical that no further comment will be made except to mention that pre-war Ford products had speedometers that were almost dead-accurate.

Summed-up, the Ford Thunderbird at $2695 is a terrific value. Our choice would be the "bare" model equipped with a 3.73 axle and three speed manual transmission without overdrive. This 3-speed manual transmission, incidently, has special close ratios; first is 2.32, second is 1.48. If only Ford would offer a good 4-speed close ratio box—it would be worth $100 extra. They might even sell a few thousand to Ford sedan buyers. ●

An early prototype car with hard top under test at the Ford proving grounds in Dearborn.

Proving Grounds Report:

THUNDERBIRD
LINCOLN
and MERCURY

Here are the complete road tests and specifications
for the three hottest cars Henry Ford ever built.

By HARVEY B. JANES

With the wheels cut hard to the right or left the Thunderbird can be driven at fairly high speed without rear wheel breakaway or excessive leaning.

IT'S A FUNNY THING how one hand washes the other in the automobile business. For over 20 years now Ford products, and especially their engines, have been the favorites among the hot-rod clan in this country. You can throw some sports-car enthusiasts into that group as well. These power-happy boys have been taking Ford, Mercury and Lincoln V-8 engines and hopping them up to what seemed to be fabulous horsepower and while the factory was mildly interested, they did very little in this direction themselves. But suddenly the entire country, in fact the world, has gone speed and horse-power crazy and what do the Ford people do? They turn around and hop the cars up at the factory and proceed to produce a line of the hottest cars ever seen on these shores. I know; I drove them.

Take the Thunderbird, for instance. We have all been hearing a lot about this car for the better part of a year and now, even though some of them have already been delivered, an air of mystery surrounds the whole conception of the vehicle. Is it or is it not a sports car? How fast is it? How does it handle? What kind of engine does it have? You've heard all these questions and more. Suppose we answer them.

Ford claims that the Thunderbird is a "personal" car, not a sports car. I, for one, agree with them. The definition of a true sports car is one that is fast, handles well, can be driven on regular roads, but can also be raced. The Thunderbird meets all of these qualifications except the last, not because Ford can't build a real sports car but because they never intended to. The Thunderbird has an engine that displaces about 4.9 liters, European style. This is not really a Ford engine, you know. It's a special Mercury job, very similar to the one in the new Montclair. Whatever it is, it pushes the car quite fast—up to nearly 120 mph—but a sports car with a 4.9-liter engine is traveling in pretty rough company. A 4.9-liter

Dashboard of the 2/3 seater is attractive, uncluttered. Instrumentation includes a tachometer which is, however, badly positioned, far off to the left. Trunk compartment is large for a "sports" car.

Author drove the car up to 100 mph with top down and windows up, found the slip stream to be very good. Optional cloth top folds behind seat.

Ferrari, for instance, can do 165 mph with ease and there are many lesser-engined unlimited cars than can top 140. Where does this put the 'bird as far as competition is concerned? Nowhere! It's not surprising, either. Most of these ultra-fast competition machines weigh under 2,500 lbs.; the Thunderbird weighs almost 3,200 or more than some low-priced sedans.

But don't get the idea that Ford's new baby is slow, because it's not. I took it out on the big banked speed track at the Ford test grounds at Dearborn, Michigan, and believe me, it was a thrill. After a few get-acquainted laps at 70 to 80 mph I began to let it have its head and it responded like an eager polo pony. There is one long straight on this track with a high bank at either end, and as I came off the first bank at the completion of one lap I put the accelerator to the floor with the speedometer just touching 70 mph. The 'bird leaped ahead instantly and began to gather speed smoothly but very, very fast. There was no wheel fight or wandering and as I went into the turn at the end of the straight I was doing just under 110 on the clock. On a shorter back stretch I was amazed to find that the car wanted to cruise at 90 mph but you'd never believe it was doing much over 60 unless you looked at the speedo. Even at 110 the car held rock-steady and there was plenty of cross wind that day in Dearborn.

When I had finished my runs on the high-speed track, I drove on into the tricky handling course that is laid out in the center of the Ford grounds. This is arranged in a series of flat but regular bends that get sharper at intervals. Starting with circles of a 300-ft. radius, they work their day down to a tight 150 ft. and they present a real test for any car's suspension and steering. I had a Ford engineer with me as I drove around and at first I took it pretty easy. The tubeless tires began to set up a steady howl at about 35 mph and I asked to have the air checked. We went back and found that two of the tires had barely 20 lbs. of pressure in them and so we promptly equalized all four wheels at 25 psi. Then we returned to the handling course. This time I didn't hear the squealing song until almost 45 mph and I began to get more confidence. I pushed faster and faster and found that, although the car does lean a bit at first, the angle doesn't increase much at speeds over 50 mph.

Thunderbird is powered—literally—by a V-8 engine that displaces 292 cu. in. That adds up to just about 4.9 liters, European style.

On the first time around the course all went well and when I hit the 300-ft.-radius turns on the second time around I was doing almost 65 mph. I kept up the same speed as the curves began to get sharper and I was starting to have a little more trouble with the steering. Then, just as I came into the 200-ft. turn, I hit a wet spot that may even have been a bit icy and suddenly the rear end was headed for the blue. I managed to correct enough to get the car in a straight line but it wouldn't stay on the road. We went off into the grass and mud, foolhardy tester and helpless engineer both tightlipped, but the car showed its stability by coming around slowly to face the road and never giving any indication that it wanted to turn over. This car, by the way, was equipped with a manual three-speed shift, and I was in second gear at the time, with my foot flat to the floor.

This momentary lapse proved one thing in a hurry:

CONTINUED ON NEXT PAGE

Lincoln's front end has been simplified, much improved. Car's greatest distinction is that it is only Ford product with old-style windshield.

Handling on this big-but-compact automobile is even finer than last year. Here it is racing around a 150-ft. circle at better than 50 mph.

the car oversteers greatly. Now some people, including Ford's top engineers, consider this an advantage but I don't—not in a car as fast as this one that tempts you to come into curves at high speed. An understeer car will drift before it breaks away and will give you something of a warning of what's about to happen. When the car starts to drift you *know* you're going too fast and you can back off on the loud pedal. A car that oversteers, however, will lose its tail first and once this happens. you have an awful lot of correcting to do to keep the car on the road. If you don't make it sometime, it might be pretty embarrassing. A certain degree of oversteer is all right for normal passenger cars but I don't care for it on the Thunderbird.

Having thoroughly frightened the engineer on the handling course I asked him to help me with the acceleration tests. He agreed and we put the car through a series of breathtaking runs with the following results: Zero to 30 averaged 4.1 seconds. Zero-to-60 time was a fast 10.4 and from there to 80 mph took another 8.6 seconds. If you don't think these are fast times, try a few corrected-time runs with your own car.

The brakes on the Thunderbird are really fine. Fast "crash" stops from 60 mph produced little fade and not much dipping either and the car will stop in a straight line with your hands off the wheel.

What are my criticisms? Well, besides the steering, I don't like the wrap-around windshield which distorts badly at the edges, acting like a lens. Even the Ford engineers admitted this. Another minor point is that I think the soft top and not the plastic hard top should come as standard equipment. The car, stripped, sells for $2,695 including a four-way power seat. If you want a cloth top instead of the hard top it costs you $70 extra, but if you want both, the charge is $270. I think most people would rather have the hard top as an option. I know I would.

WHEN I climbed behind the wheel of the new Lincoln Capri I got still another thrill. Basically the same as last year's model but with some engine and chassis modifications, this car gives the impression of being expensive

Beautiful Lincoln Capri can hold its own style-wise and performance-wise with any car in America. In stock form it approaches 110 mph.

Here's what the tricky Ford handling course looks like through the windshield of a Lincoln at speed. Tight curves are left unbanked.

Push-button lubrication, operated from inside the car, is optional on 1955 Lincolns, Mercurys. Oil reservoir is under hood, as shown.

but not gaudy. It is the only automobile in the Ford line that does not have a wrap-around windshield and this pleased me, as you may have guessed it would. It does have a new wrap-around bumper, though, and a few other styling innovations that make for real class.

But the big question to me was "how does it drive?" So I took it around the same route that I had followed with the Thunderbird. Toward the end of my third lap on the speed track, as I neared that same last turn leading into the straight, I held the needle at 70 mph, just as I had done with the 'bird. Believe it or not, this car was actually faster than the other bomb had been from 70 to 100 mph. I got it up to an indicated 115 by the end of that straight and although the Lincoln won't match the Thunderbird for top speed, it will climb right up to almost 110 mph, and with no dead spots in acceleration. The answer, of course, is torque, which is a factor of just plain engine size. The big Lincoln V-8 puts out 225 hp this year and develops 332 ft./lbs. of torque at 2,500 rpm. The Thunderbird's torque rating is 286 ft./lbs. at that same 2,500 rpm. That's where the difference in dig comes from.

On the handling course the Lincoln showed me why it has won its class in the Mexican Road Race three years

Clever use of chromium on the Capri minimizes the "slab-sided" effect, makes the car appear more graceful. Wrap-around bumper is new.

CONTINUED ON NEXT PAGE

Two-door Mercury Custom is one of the least expensive cars in the line. Power is supplied by a new 188-hp V-8 engine that pushes it over 100 mph.

Mercury performed well on the speed track, got up over 100 mph with ease. Banked turns could be negotiated at 85 mph without any strain.

Dashboard has all instruments grouped in a V-shaped panel in front of the driver. The big speedometer goes up to an indicated 120 mph.

running. This is a superb handling automobile—beautifully balanced with fine, accurate steering and the best front suspension of any American car I have ever driven. On the small 150-ft. circle the Lincoln went around under perfect control at speeds up to 55 mph. This kind of stability and feel, plus all the luxury Lincoln has to offer, is going to be mighty hard to beat.

An interesting fact that most people don't realize about the Mexican thing incidentally, is that this past race was won by 1954 Lincolns, not the brand new models. Race rules state that the year of the cars in competition must correspond with the year the race is run. This is to make sure that one manufacturer doesn't get an unfair advantage by jumping the gun with his new models. Just thought you'd like to know.

Getting on with the test, I went into the usual acceleration runs but since it had rained in the meantime I would prefer not to give my exact figures since they would be neither accurate nor fair. I will say, though, that the 1955 Lincoln Capri will

Interiors are brightly colored and beautifully designed. A combination of heavy plastic and fine fabrics should prove quite durable.

Here is the Montclair—the glamour car in this year's Mercury line. With its all-new styling and high speed it may become 1955's most popular car.

Thunderbird, Lincoln and Mercury

surely get to 30 mph in under 4.5 seconds and to 60 in under 12. And when you do tromp on the gas, you get an even surge of power transmitted through Lincoln's brand new Turbodrive automatic gearbox. This is a torque-converter unit similar to the ones in the Thunderbird and the new Merc that is coupled to a three-speed planetary gearbox and it gives acceleration so smooth you almost can't believe it. First-gear starts are possible without having to put the lever in low manually. All you do is floorboard the accelerator and the car takes off like a bomb in first and up-shifts to second at full throttle. If you take off in a calmer fashion, you start in second which is not slow either. Any way you look at it, it's a real smoothie.

In spite of its big, powerful engine, the Lincoln should be an economical car. Last year's model, with 205 hp, was good for up to 18 mpg on the open road and gas mileage should be even better this year despite the horsepower increase. The reason is that the standard rear-axle ratio has been changed from 3.31 to 3.07. This is a wise move on Lincoln's part; it will make more difference in gas mileage than it will in acceleration. The 20 extra horses will see to that.

Standard equipment on all new Lincolns are tubeless tires—which seem to be taking the industry by storm—and twin exhausts. Prices for the Capri run from about $3,800 to $4,100 at the factory. If I had that kind of loot to spend on a car, I'd think twice before I bought anything else.

FROM the Lincoln I jumped right into a new Mercury Montclair—which may well turn out to be the sleeper of the year. It's hot as a pistol and roomier and better-looking even than the Capri (except for that you-know-what windshield). Back we went onto the giant soup-bowl track and here I got my first start. The car I was testing was so new it didn't even have all of its chromium on, which was fine with me except that it did look a bit naked. Anyway, there hadn't been too much care put into the body assembly because the car was only a test-grounds model. While I was circling the outside track at 85 mph with one of the company men, I suddenly heard a loud clattering noise as we came off one of the high banks. It was gone in a moment but I was sort of concerned.

"Don't worry," said the engineer, smiling. "It's only a hub cap."

I smiled back, wondering what was going to fall off next, but nothing did. In fact I kept smiling and the Merc took me up to an honest 103 mph just because I was so nice. Here again, there was no flat spot in acceleration and the car seemed so fast that I was anxious to run off timed tests.

So we did that next, before the handling and braking shakedown. And was I glad. Hang onto your hats, boys, because here is a rough idea of what a well-tuned 198-hp. Montclair can do: Zero to 30 mph took only 4.3 seconds, just two-tenths of a second slower than the Thunderbird! And that's not all. Zero to 60 time was 11.4 seconds, just one second behind the 'Bird with exactly the same engine (unofficially), and zero to 80 mph ran 20.7 seconds. These figures are all the more amazing when you consider that the Montclair is a full-sized sedan, weighing at least 350 lbs. more than the Thunderbird!

Still shaking my head in disbelief, I staggered back into the car after a brief rest period and headed for my old pal, the handling course. Here again the Merc performed like a slightly smaller Lincoln and I felt a definite advantage from the four inches less of wheelbase. The steering didn't have quite the positive feel of the Lincoln, but all the cars tested were early production-line models and the difference might just have been in individual cars. There was some body roll but nothing excessive and certainly not enough to affect control under ordinary driving conditions. If you want to go like a racing driver, you'll have to stiffen up the suspension of any American automobile.

Just as with the Lincoln, standard rear-axle ratios have been changed this year, from 3.54 to 3.15 on all Mercomatic cars.. And for the same reason as is true for the Lincoln, this will give a slight increase in gas mileage, in spite of the added horsepower. Speaking of Mercomatic, this year's version is better than ever and just about as smooth as Lincoln's new automatic transmission, with the same kick-down feature. Downshifts can be made into "low," by the way, at speeds over 50 mph, a useful factor for additional braking power.

Not that the Mercury needs any more braking power under normal use. I couldn't get it to show any fade at all and you shouldn't have any trouble either, unless you drive down from the top of Pike's Peak three or four times a day.

By now you may have gotten the impression that I like the Mercury. That would be an understatement. I love its looks, visibility, speed and handling. The available color schemes are startlingly brilliant, to say the least, but mostly in fine taste, and the interiors are cheerful and practical. I even like the new "frenched" headlight treatment that is featured on the entire Ford line. Every feature of these cars should be very popular, from their dual exhausts right on up. But don't let me be a salesman; go drive them yourself. You can walk away with a new Mercury for less than $3,000. It's something to think about.●

THUNDERBIRD SPECIFICATIONS

ENGINE: V-8, overhead valves; bore, 3.75 in.; stroke, 3.30 in.; total displacement, 292 cu. in.; developed hp, 193 with standard transmission, 198 with Fordomatic, both at 4,400 rpm; compression ratio, 8.1 to 1 conventional, 8.5 to 1 with Fordomatic; maximum torque, 286 ft./lbs. at 2,500 rpm; four-throat carburetor; ignition, 6 volts.
TRANSMISSION: three-speed manual or Fordomatic torque converter with three planetary gears; overdrive (opt.)
REAR AXLE RATIO: conventional. 3.73; overdrive, 3.92; Fordomatic, 3.31.
SUSPENSION: front, independent ball-joint coil spring system with two transverse control arms of unequal length; rear, semi-elliptic leaf springs with rubber-bushed shackles.
BRAKES: four-wheel hydraulic, internal expanding; 11-in.-diameter drums; power booster available.
DIMENSIONS: wheelbase, 102 in.; tread (front and rear), 56 in.; width, 70 in.; height, 52 in.; over-all length, 175 in.; turning circle, 36 ft.; weight, 3,150 lbs.; tires, tubeless, 6.70 x 15. (6.00 x 16 optional.)

LINCOLN CAPRI SPECIFICATIONS

ENGINE: V-8, overhead valves; bore, 3.94 in.; stroke, 3.50 in.; total displacement, 341 cu. in.; developed hp, 225 at 4,400 rpm; maximum torque, 332 ft./lbs. at 2,500 rpm; compression ratio, 8.5 to 1; four-throat carburetor; ignition, 6 volt.
TRANSMISSION: Turbo-drive torque converter with three planetary gears.
REAR AXLE RATIO: 3.31 standard; 3.07 with air-conditioning.
SUSPENSION: front, independent ball-joint coil-spring system; rear, semi-elliptic leaf springs.
BRAKES: four-wheel hydraulic, internal expanding; 12-in.-diameter drums; power booster available.
DIMENSIONS: wheelbase, 123 in.; front tread, 58.5 in.; rear tread, 60 in.; width, 77.6 in.; height, 62.7 in.; over-all length, 215.6 in.; turning circle, 45.7 ft.; weight, 4,300 lbs. (approx.); tires, tubeless, 8.00 x 15.

MERCURY MONTCLAIR SPECIFICATIONS

ENGINE: V-8, overhead valves; bore, 3.75 in.; stroke, 3.30 in.; total displacement, 292 cu. in.; developed hp, 198 at 4,400 rpm; maximum torque, 286 ft./lbs. at 2,500 rpm; compression ratio, 8.5 to 1; four-throat carburetor; ignition, 6 volt.
TRANSMISSION: Mercomatic torque converter with three planetary gears; standard three-speed manual and overdrive available.
REAR AXLE RATIO: conventional, 3.73; overdrive, 4.09; Mercomatic, 3.15.
SUSPENSION: front, independent ball-joint coil-spring system; rear, semi-elliptic leaf springs.
BRAKES: four-wheel hydraulic, internal expanding; 11-in.-diameter drums.
DIMENSIONS: wheelbase, 119 in.; front tread, 58 in.; rear tread, 59 in.; width, 76.4 in.; height, 58.6 in.; over-all length, 206.3 in.; turning circle, 42.8 ft.; weight, not available; tires, tubeless, 7.60 x 15.

BENJAMIN WEST and Bill Lloyd look over the latter's new Thunderbird. Modifications have been made to the lighting, dampers, brake linings and ignition. Styling is pleasantly restrained by American standards.

BENJAMIN WEST,

Technical Editor of

a leading U.S. motoring

journal, tests for AUTOSPORT

America's new sports car, the

Ford Thunderbird

SLIGHTLY over two years ago, the Ford Motor Company sent out confidential questionnaires to all Ford dealers on the subject of a sports car for the American car buyer. Dealers were asked primarily if such a car would sell and further, what should it entail where seating, luggage space and other sales points were concerned?

Concrete answers were few, but none the less, Ford designated chassis engineers to the project "sportscar". Soon thereafter, coachwork designers were invited to submit drawings to fit a Fordlike prototype box X frame and interestingly enough, Ford's own craftsmen won the final style choice by an impartial board of judges. The 102 ins. wheelbase by 56 ins. track chassis then was refined to fit both body and its Mercury V8 192 h.p. engine and other stock components, the resulting 3,000 lb. car being named the Thunderbird, perhaps in honour of the ancient bird god of American Indian tribes.

I have just finished compiling much first hand information on some newly delivered Thunderbird cars which I have obtained from their owners in my Connecticut area. These owners include, among others, William Lloyd, co-winner of Sebring 1954, Sherwood Johnston, Cunningham team driver, and Briggs Cunningham himself.

I have driven a number of the cars and tried both the Fordomatic automatic gearbox and the very good 3-speed con-ventional box equipped with overdrive in top and second gears.

As none of these cars is more than a few weeks old, I have been extremely fortunate in having Lloyd's well broken-in car as a test vehicle. Lloyd is the first Thunderbird owner in the East, ordering his car last April and finally obtaining it in November, the day before the Southern Apallachian Rally. He drove his Bird, as the cars are now nick-named, throughout the event with no trouble and then travelled to Florida for top speed runs, returning to his Fairfield home with a total mileage reading over 4,000 in just six days.

Later, Lloyd arranged a test competition event between three Birds and two M-type (modified) Jaguars. Held at the Thompson, Connecticut race course during December, the event was organized as fairly as possible with Lloyd, Sherwood Johnston and Gordon Lipe (all top S.C.C.A. race drivers) pitting their Birds against George Constantine, twice winner at Watkins Glen, and Richard Perrin, another first placer, both piloting their well-known proven M-Jaguars.

The cars were lined up with Lloyd, Perrin and Lipe in the front row, and with Johnston and Constantine in second row. A very good start was made and all cars left the line evenly and held position while accelerating. Within half a mile, however, both Jaguars swept through a tight downhill turn to gain a car length lead over the Birds. This lead was increased to several lengths upon the next bend, a tight U following a half mile straight.

As I was trailing the contestants in a friend's Jaguar, I could clearly observe that all Birds floated upon severe braking with over-light rear springing much in evidence. Once into the curve and during acceleration on smooth surfaces providing good traction, the Birds held their own very well. Entering the curves, breakaway occurred very early and evenly on all four wheels and it appears that tracking of these cars through bends at any speed without sliding is a virtual impossibility due to present suspension, weight distribution, and perhaps the stock tubeless tyres which have rather rigid sidewalls and cold-rubber treads.

With my Jaguar pulled off course after the first lap, I watch three more laps in which the M-Jaguars drew further ahead until almost half a mile was between them and Lloyd's most hotly pursuing Bird. As no further test was required, all Birds pulled up at the paddock and their owners commented on the need for better dampers and stronger rear springs, saying, none-the-less, that the cars had no vices and were good fun. Lloyd's car had given way, he told us, because of a grabbing right rear brake and indeed, all the Birds' brakes were smoking nicely. I drove in Lloyd's car shortly after this and marvelled that he kept up, for a grease leak had caused a very nasty condition on the linings.

I must here point out that the Ford people say that these cars are not primarily designed for racing . . . if one could have so called this gentlemanly tilt of vehicles, and the Birds do tilt considerably on corners. So a very fine show was made, especially when it is

★

SLEEK and unornamented, the lines of the Thunderbird are well shown here. The 6½-inch ground clearance is unexpected in a car of this type.

★

COCKPIT VIEW shows the stubby central gear lever and the large speedometer flanked by tachometer and clock. There is no shortage of leg-room!

realized that Lipe's car cornered admirably with power-assisted steering and lost little ground with Fordomatic transmission.

Following the lappery came a most carefully timed quarter mile sprint event on the back stretch with about a 2 per cent. upgrade. Best time was 16.8 secs. for Johnston's Bird which trailed Constantine's M-Jaguar by only one-tenth of a sec. The Fordomatic was clocked at 17.2 secs.

So enough with tooth-for-tooth testing; let's look at Birds from the ladies' viewpoint a moment. A charming lady neighbour of medium dimensions received a bright red Bird for Christmas. (Birds come in red, light blue and black enamels.) She has much praise to offer plus a small complaint. Says the two seats are true dream-car plastic with matching red borders on white centre, but the white soils swiftly, the plastic grows quite slack when warm and what's a bit more annoying, the seat is too smooth for comfort. For it seems the bench is lacking in sufficient thigh grip during sudden stops and that she, when passenger, has landed in a heap under the facia on several occasions. She is short, her husband tall, and the fascinating electric push buttons on the door panel cause the entire bench to move fore or aft, up or down, as a thing of wonder, but, so far, Ford provides no automatic foot brace for dainty passengers. So she drives!

Two cranks of a chrome handle lowers the side window, or push buttons for the task may be purchased optionally. And, if demanded, two small streams of water play upon the huge 1,027 sq. ins. area shatterproof windscreen of "wraparound" design. The two wipers are of the vacuum-with-booster type and are very good, clearing efficiently even in cloudbursts, but they cannot clean the "wrapped around" side areas which consequently get pretty blind at times. The wrap or bend point of the screen causes delightful undulations in all scenery observed therethrough, but one does not mind this much and I rejoiced in the lack of any light reflections within the cockpit by day or night.

The speedometer reads up to 150 m.p.h. and protrudes above the convex rounded fibre crash panel. Lloyd's car is optimistic by 12 per cent. on this needle and by 2 per cent. on the odometer. But another car showed a speed

dial fully 18 per cent. pessimistic . . . something quite rare! A small tachometer is mounted to left of the stock Ford speedometer instrument cluster, and tells the truest tale with approximately 22 m.p.h. for each 1,000 r.p.m. in top gear.

Lloyd's car, with overdrive engaged, will do a real 123 m.p.h. and has more power on hand. But tubeless tyres being not recommended for high speeds, it was felt safer to explore no higher altitudes. One hundred m.p.h. may be obtained within 25 secs. from rest, whereupon the zoom rate falls gently off.

The short throw, three-speed box is a positive delight with spring-loaded first for sure, fast upshifts into second. The dry, single-plate clutch has a woven rather than moulded lining which provides very ladylike action. First gear is not synchro, but I flipped down into it via double declutch at some 20 or more m.p.h., time and again, with no dire results. The whole box sounds and feels solid, very like that of the Lincoln, and is most right for our crowded highways, providing amazing top gear flexibility though I'd say undergeared for open roads unless overdrive is used. Ratios are 2.32 to 1 in first, 1.48 to 1 in second, 1 to 1 in top and overdrive is 0.70 to 1. Rear axle ratios are 3.73 to 1 stock; 3.92 to 1 overdrive; 3.31 to 1 Fordomatic.

The Borg-Warner overdrive reduces

engine speed by 30 per cent. and is engaged by momentarily backing off on the throttle when the car speed exceeds 27 m.p.h. Direct drive may be kicked-in at any speed over 27 m.p.h. by "flooring the gas". The unit free-wheels when speeds drop below 21 m.p.h. and can be locked on or off by a T lever below the facia. I found the second gear overdrive a wonderful 80 m.p.h. affair and understand that the kick-in switch may be relocated from beneath the throttle to atop the gear lever for handiness.

Next is the Fordomatic, a torque converter with three planetary gears, as designed for Birds. The control column is located where the conventional gear lever belongs, on the floor to the driver's right. It acts with an in-line throw, fore to aft positions being PARK, REVERSE, NEUTRAL, HI, LO. Atop the column's large ballgrip is a flush-fitted safety button which, upon partial squeeze-down, permits engagement of LO and REVERSE. Full squeeze is needed to engage PARK.

The HI position will engage a 2.40:1 gear for takeoff, and if the throttle is floored from there on, a 1.47:1 gear pops in at about 34 m.p.h. followed by a 1:1 top gear at 65 m.p.h. Backing off a bit on the throttle will permit the next higher gear to engage at speeds below the peak shift points or if sufficient load is imposed at speeds below the peak shift settings, the corresponding lower gears are engaged. Thus, rather unexpected down or up shifts may occur while cornering.

To avoid such impromptu changing, a formula not given in the Ford manual follows. At all speeds above 28 m.p.h. the LO position permits engagement of the 1.47:1 gear and uninterrupted torque for faster cornering, braking and so on. But, should one drop below 28 m.p.h. and then accelerate, even slightly, the 2.40:1 is permanently engaged in LO. So, you sneak into HI to avoid overrevs and then back into LO when above 28 m.p.h. for a useful second gear once more. I mislaid this formula once and found Lipe's engine did not burst at over 5,000 r.p.m. in bottom gear, for which we were both thankful.

Now the engine department, which as you can see, is quite fine. The 1955 Mercury V8 block with o.h.v. is just under 5 litres at 292 cubic inch capacity. Bore is 3.75 ins., stroke 3.30. Compression is stock 8.1:1, or 8.5:1 with

★

FLYING SAUCER? The large aircleaner conceals the four-choke Holley carburetter. The power unit is basically a V8 Mercury of nearly 5 litres.

★

Fordomatic; 193 or 198 h.p., respectively. The 198 h.p. is rated at 4,400 r.p.m. 286 ft. lb. torque is at 2,500 r.p.m.

I here thank Gordon Lipe for the test fact that 112 h.p. comes to the Fordomatic rear wheels at 4,100 r.p.m. Also that an 80 h.p. load may be imposed at 110 m.p.h. Both figures were obtained on a Clayton dynamometer freshly strobe-calibrated and supervised by a Clayton engineer.

Huddled under an impressive chrome disc aircleaner (that looks *just* like a Martian visitor's craft) lies the four-throat carburetter with its second-string venturis of vacuum-actuated design. These booster venturis are most evident upon heavy-footed driving, the car feeling as though a lower gear had been engaged when they cut in. These carburetters give fine mileage with U.S. gallons consumed at rates varying from 17 m.p.g. city driving to almost 25 m.p.g. on open highways at 60 to 75 m.p.h. speeds . . . in overdrive cars.

The innards of Birds' engines are said to be stock, although we understand the crankshaft is specially designed for full-torque oil flow and the rods are drilled with two oil squirt holes. And speaking of oil, the good Ford Thunderbird manual warns that the telltale oil pressure light may blink after sudden stops and that one mustn't worry. Just for fun, a real oil pressure gauge was installed on Lloyd's car and we wonder just where the pressure does go to on severe braking? So far, it has always returned to normal and has not caused damage at higher engine speeds. And another thing, the new engines do burn oil quite a bit but this is to be calculated with the tin-plated aluminium pistons and three iron rings (top and oil rings chrome plated) which, once seated, provide proper oil sealing. Lloyd's car

ACCELERATION GRAPH
OF
FORD THUNDERBIRD

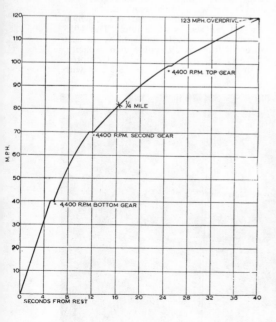

Specification and Performance

Cars tested: Ford "Thunderbird" 2-seater convertible coupés (five examples), price in U.S.A. $3,450 with synchromesh gearbox, automatic seat adjustment and standard tubeless tyres. Cars with all optional equipment except steel hardtop, $3,993.

Engine: Mercury 8-cylinder vee, 95.25 mm. x 83.82 mm. (4,785 c.c.). Overhead valves operated by pushrods, 4-choke Holley carburetter, automatic choke, vacuum-operated booster venturis, 198 b.h.p. at 4,400 r.p.m., 8.5:1 compression ratio (Fordomatic version).

Transmission: (manual) 3-speed gearbox with synchromesh on second and top and central control. Gearbox ratios: 2.32, 1.48 and 1:1. Borg-Warner overdrive, 0.70:1. Single-dry-plate clutch with woven lining, area 113.1 sq. in. (Fordomatic) single-stage, 3-element torque converter with air-cooled planetary gears. Automatic second gear engagement and automatic low gear start on full throttle. Selector lever on floor in centre of cockpit. Hotchkiss final drive with tubular propeller shaft. Rear axle ratios: manual, 3.73:1; with overdrive, 3.92:1; with Fordomatic, 3.31:1.

Chassis: Box section side members, X-braced. Independent front suspension with helical springs and unequal-length wishbones. Worm-type steering box. Symmetrically divided track rod. Semi-elliptic springs at rear. Bolt-on steel disc wheels with 6.70 x 15 in. tubeless tyres. Bendix hydraulic duo-servo brakes with 11 ins. dia. drums. Riveted-on moulded linings, total area 175.46 sq. ins. Effectiveness, 60 per cent. front, 40 per cent. rear. Optional extras: power-assisted steering, booster brakes.

Equipment: 6-volt lighting and starting. Speedometer, odometer, tachometer, water temperature and fuel gauges, warning lights for oil pressure and charging rate, clock. Flasher-type direction indicators. Vacuum-with-booster screen wipers. Radio. Electric seat adjustment. Optional extras: Electric window winders, screen washers, steel hardtop, "engine dress-up kit" (chrome fan, etc.), rear wheel spats, snap-on wheel covers to simulate wire wheels.

Dimensions: Wheelbase, 102 ins.; track, 56 ins.; overall length, 175.3 ins.; width, 70.3 ins.; height (hood erected), 52.4 ins.; ground clearance, 6.5 ins.; turning circle, 36 ft.; dry weight, 3,014 lb.; curb weight, 3,160 lb. (with overdrive); weight distribution, equal front and rear.

Performance: Maximum speed reached in tests, 123 m.p.h. Higher speed was not attempted as stock tubeless tyres were in use. Acceleration: 0-30 m.p.h., 3.5 secs.; 0-50, 7 secs.; 0-60, 8.8 secs.; 0-70, 11.5 secs.; 0-80, 15.9 secs.; 0-90, 20.0 secs.; 0-100, 25.8 secs.; 0-110, 32.8 secs.; 0-120, 41.0 secs.; 0-123, 45.0 secs.

Fuel consumption: approx. 18 m.p.g. (U.S. gallons).

has now run 6,000 miles and no longer burns oil.

Coming up from the quite accessible engine room (unless you've ordered all the power stuff) we'll look at the Birds' steering design. That 20.1 to 1 ratio with 3.4 turns lock-to-lock isn't bad when you remember that these cars oversteer in a manner befitting some venerable veterans long thought *passé*. The helm itself is 17 ins. in diameter and adjusts fore and aft with 3 ins. travel *à la* Jaguar. I don't like the half horn ring so close to the wheel rim when fast handling is needed, but bless 'em for omitting that nasty big Jag-type centre blow button, anyway!

Front suspension is most obviously of Lincoln origin. Linkage consists of a worm and two-tooth roller which actuates the drop-arm aft-linked to equal length tie rods. The Ford "ball joint" method of front top A-arm hookup is standard and I will always worry about this single link being subject to the severe brake torque shocks found in fast competition after one front wheel slides, as on an oil patch.

I imagine that this ball joint is really strong enough and know that Ford has reason to rely on it if only by virtue of some unexpected tests which occurred during the Birds' development. I'm told that originally all four Bendix 11-inch diameter hydraulic brakes were fitted with 2¼ ins. width shoes which self-energized themselves into nasty fits of locking full on. The Ford way out was to nip a half inch from the leading primary shoe width, leaving the secondary shoe full original width. Thus the present new brakes have excellent action with their total of 175.46 sq. ins. area, but what sort of wear will occur on the iron drums? The riveted-on linings are stock moulded asbestos which takes a large amount of abuse before fading away rather permanently. And one can pull up in about 118 ft. from 60 m.p.h. on good smooth-surface roads where traction is tops. Jaguars will do this in 111 ft., if we remember our own last year's tests.

Power brakes are available but I can't say that Birds need them and one try-out proved them so dangerously sensitive that I would personally never drive such a device.

The current stock Ford 30-70-acting telescopic shock-absorbers are of 1 in. diameter and located within the coil springs . . . and at an angle up-inwards to the frame cross member ahead of the rear axle. I understand Ford now contemplates offering their heavier four-position adjustable dampers as later-on equipment, which is a good idea.

The nylon black top fits snugly, looks very neat and lifts completely from the body shell to be hand stowed behind the seatback. This is an operation no more difficult than that on a Jaguar. Once up, the hood keeps the worst torrents of rain outside and does not rattle in the slightest. Furthermore, it stays put at full bore.

And novel indeed is the new steel accessory top which may be lifted off completely for summer driving as usual with the stock nylon. This razor-edge styled top was originally scheduled in plastic but, as usual under extremes of climate testing, the plastic simply would never fit on.

Perhaps the best indication that this Bird may be honestly classed sports is the completely hopeless lack of luggage space. The same lady who had trouble staying on the seat grew desperate also upon trying to transport her weekly wash hamper, either in the boot or the cockpit. She almost gave the car up, but her very intelligent husband took her round for a day's looking at the other new but conventional cars. That did it. And straps now hold the large hamper fast to an opened boot.

So I think I can wind up this accounting on a happy note. With a road clearance of full 6.5 ins., width of 70.3 ins. and overall length of 175.3 ins., this smooth riding Thunderbird can go anywhere comfortably and in high style. Ford has built the best U.S. sports car going . . . and it will truly go!

T-Bird Makes Its Bid

Although billed as a "personal" car, this sleek machine is being run in competition events

Veteran IMCA driver Herschel Buchanan entered a T-Bird in a stock car race this spring at the Shreveport (La.) Fairgrounds.

By WILLIAM LEE

WHEN the Ford Thunderbird flew into the arms of a waiting public last year, the publicists from Dearborn, Mich., almost knocked themselves out in trying to knock down the idea that the sleek little beauty was a sports car. And, above all, they were more than anxious to dispel any rumor that the high-powered job could be used for racing.

But despite Ford's horror of building up the T-Bird as a competition car, hard cash is still good in the dealer showrooms and many stock and sports car race drivers wanted a chance to see if the machinery had enough ambition and control for racing. Within a few months, Dearborn's "personal car" really was living up to its name, but in personal

competition. In almost every race in which the T-Bird has appeared, it's been a battle of the field against the newcomer.

So far, it's been a personal affront to the Thunderbird. With a 198 hp. engine and a neat gear ratio, the matter of acceleration is almost fantastic even when compared to Buicks, Oldsmobiles, Hudsons, Jaguars, Austin-Healeys and other leading stock and sports cars. Coming out of a turn, the T-Bird goes like a striped ape, but going into the turns, it sometimes resembles a healthy duck on the way to lay an egg. Ford was right when it tried to avoid the sports car concept of the T-Bird. The suspension and steering just aren't there. But, oddly, neither does it handle like a straight Detroit stock product. This

in-between business may be the seat of the trouble—and it also may be the reason why the T-Bird possesses enough potential to become the terror of the stock car circuits.

First, the Thunderbird *is* a stock car. Manufactured under a semblance of mass production, it qualifies for that category. Second, it has enough under the hood to make it a husky threat to any competitor, large or small. At Daytona Beach Speed Week, the T-Bird contingent staged quite a show with 120 mph.-plus runs. Only the Chrysler 300s could show better speeds in the stock car class.

Then, what's wrong with the Thunderbird? Why is it running into so much trouble, both in sports car and stock

This is what happened to Buchanan's T-Bird; a snapped axle flange put the Bird out of race and Mr. Buchanan in hospital.

racing? So far, it hasn't been impressive. Let's look at its record in a few performances this year.

In February, the T-Bird tried its wings at Sebring, Fla., and at Willow Springs, Calif. The tight turns of the Florida 12-hour Grand Prix of Endurance were too much. After all, acceleration can be carried only so far. Eventually, even the fastest car must depend on suspension and steering to get it around the course. In the Sebring business, the Thunderbird finished 37th overall and seventh in its class. Unfortunately, the Ford product fell into Class C—the same in which the Jaguars (including the Type D) fell. While Phil Walters and Mike Hawthorn in the D-Jag completed 182 laps to win, the Thunderbird was confined to a 138-lap total. But, to Ford's credit, a large array of potent machinery was hard-pressed to push the T-Bird down into such a lowly finishing position. Jags, Ferraris, Maseratis, Austin-Healeys, Oscas, Porsches and Siatas finished ahead. The much-touted Mercedes-Benz 300SL put one car in 21st place and a second finished in 35th, only two spots above the Thunderbird.

At Willow Springs, the stock model Thunderbird ran into trouble because of its new tubeless tires—a stock item on the car. With a pebble between the rim and tire, the T-Bird was losing air on every turn and inside of a few turns, the flattening tire snapped it into a spin, thereby ending the effort to win.

Last March, the stock car racing enthusiasts were treated to a bit more than expected at Shreveport, La. A veteran of almost 25 years in IMCA big car and stock racing, Herschel Buchanan, put a brand-new T-Bird into the Gulf States Championship contest and almost put himself out of competition—permanently.

In one of its first serious bids for racing honors among the stock cars, the Thunderbird cleaned up the time trials.

The time was 31.67 seconds for the half-mile track—approximately 57 mph. On the 15-lap first heat, Buchanan cut a neat 8:12.54 average.

The only serious competition encountered by the T-Bird came from a 1955 Olds 88 piloted by "Wild Bill" Harrison of Topeka, Kans. Buchanan and Harrison went at it like a pair of Kilkenny cats when the flag fell. It was a strange spectacle, in some ways. The low, sleek lines of the Bird was ruined by the roll bars installed under IMCA rules, but the change in ap-

pearance probably saved Buchanan from ruin. From the start, Buchanan appeared to be in trouble with the steering department. The car had been delivered to him only three days before the race and perhaps he had lacked time to become fully acquainted with the machinery.

Buchanan, always rides high on the turns, a holdover from his work in the big cars. On two occasions during the race, he brushed the wall with the T-Bird, apparently unable to hold it down. But, he led the race for 54

Although many sports car drivers are using the Thunderbird with the top off, the stockers prefer to employ the hardtop model- always with roll bars added.

laps and regained it on the 61st time around. In the 70th lap, he was leading Harrison by less than 20 feet when an axle flange snapped. The T-Bird settled on its right rear fender, rebounded about 15 feet straight up and made a complete flip to land on the roll bars. The detachable top detached itself on the first flip and sailed into the wide blue yonder. Buchanan rolled sideways several times before ending the race with serious injuries.

At the risk of second guessing a foregone conclusion, many experts felt that the T-Bird would have roosted high on the tree that day if mechanical trouble had not clipped its feathers.

Later in the spring, the Sports Car Owners and Drivers Association, a renegade (by Sports Car Club of America mores) outfit which likes the sight of long green better than small trophies, staged an affair at the Weatherly and Sawyer Speedway, Virginia Beach, Va. A Thunderbird was among the entries, driven by Nick Cavaluzzi of Long Island, N. Y. When qualifying trials began, it was a reasonable bet that Cavaluzzi was in for trouble on the tight half-mile course. Competing against Jaguars, Austin-Healeys and MGs, the T-Bird again demonstrated its ability to go like a rabbit out of the turns and like an overfed washerwoman into them.

Cavaluzzi finished *third* with a Healey copping the cash and an MG second. Analysis of the Bird's performance followed the preset pattern—not a sports car and still, not a stock car.

With this "neither fish nor fowl" brand, where does the T-Bird fit into the racing picture? Will the Dearborn publicity boys win their fight to sell the beautiful little car as a "personal" machine without merit as a competition model?

Members of the SPEED AGE staff have driven the Thunderbird and they report the following:

Acceleration equals—or surpasses—almost any sports car under the Ferrari-Maserati-Mercedes class. On the straightaway, the thing handles beautifully until it enters the 75-85 mph. bracket, and above. Then, the entire business seems to wander off in search of other fields, and, unless there's a nice, flat field handy, you may find yourself in serious trouble. The front end expresses a strong desire to plane and the rear is embarrassingly obvious in its wish to overtake the front. Steering is just as described—not tight enough for a sports car and too tight for a stock model. Suspension is the same. The entire affair offers a nice challenge to a driver. He has a choice of a loose sports car or a reasonably tight stock job—dependent on where he races.

But, with 198 horses and a beautiful hunk of torque in the mechanical division, the Bird certainly is a challenge. It can't beat a Jag or a Healey, day in and day out, but it's going to make a lot of stock cars look sick—when the right drivers find the right combination. Airlift shocks, driver adjustment to the

The potent Thunderbird engine develops 198 horsepower and, combined with the neat gear ratio, the Bird is a competitor's dream when it comes to acceleration.

steering and a general "beefing up" of wheels and running gear will find it in front of most Detroit models.

It may not win many races this year, since few new cars do, but look out

boys. Next season, you may be looking at the classy rear end of a T-Bird as it crosses the line ahead of you. It's all a matter of where you're going to sit.

•

This little baby could have taken it all at Virginia Beach if it had not been for "neither fish nor fowl" steering and suspension, which was too hard to handle.

SALUTE TO THE
THUNDERBIRD

It's more than just a matter of speed and styling—after nearly a year of solid success, it amounts to the acceptance of a genuinely new idea in cars that'll influence the shape of things to come

IN AN industry where conservative imitation is a rule that's rarely broken, the Ford Motor Company has come up with what can only be called a revolution in personal transportation. The product of this revolution is the Ford Thunderbird.

The Thunderbird is a new kind of car. It was not designed to appeal to the die-hard devotees of spartan, high-performance machinery, and it is a far cry from the traditional shake, rattle, and roll sports job. Instead, it has looks, luxury, and most of the conveniences of the bulky automotive palaces in the upper price bracket.

Still, few experts deny that in concept, performance and style, the T-Bird is in the sports car class. Even the purist fan magazines that specialize in the drawing of fine distinctions between sports and pseudo-sports machines agree that its claim to the adjective is legitimate. About the only authority that has *not* labelled the T-Bird a sports car is the Ford Motor Company itself.

Ford prefers to call it a "personal" car, and with good reason. In the first place, many of the dream cars displayed to the public in recent years have also been called "sports" cars. The experts guffawed, but more important, most of the solid citizenry yawned. Furthermore, there is a vast body of American car-buyers that is convinced that sports cars are for eccentrics. Most of them wouldn't buy a Ferrari even if it cost as little as the Thunderbird. The "sports" label would not be likely to intrigue them. But a car that was "personal"—and therefore distinctive and desirable—would.

Ford's reasoning has been borne out by the results. Middle-aged matrons think the T-Bird is the cutest thing they've ever seen. The business executive whose boss might glower if he suddenly appeared in the cockpit of a hairy, all-out sports car, becomes no less respectable at the wheel of a Thunderbird. And ownership of a T-Bird is acutely craved by tens of thousands of Americans who want a spirited, precise, high-performance touring machine of nearly all-around utility.

The Thunderbird is the first American car which has

CONTINUED ON PAGE 53

DRIVERS REPORT

TWO SUPERCHARGED T-BIRDS

TWO of the most persistent rumors from Detroit concern the 1956 Ford Thunderbird; one says it will appear with fuel injection, the other maintains the McCulloch supercharger will be optional equipment. Either or both these reports may or may not be true. However, quite a number of Thunderbird owners are having the blowers installed on the 1955 models with performance results that are exceptionally interesting.

In view of all this, an invitation of Paxton Industries (the sales division of

McCulloch Motors) to test drive a compressor-equipped T-Bird was accepted. While the investigation did not assume the proportions of a comprehensive road test, a fifth wheel and Weston electric speedo was used to insure accuracy.

Two Thunderbirds were taken out on a straight stretch of pavement for acceleration tests. One had a Fordomatic transmission, the other carried the overdrive unit. Speedometer corrections were made first and disclosed the following: at indicated 30. mph, 45 mph and 60 mph, the respective actual speeds were 26 mph, 38 mph and 50 mph. Each of the cars, incidentally, were well broken in by thousands of road miles.

It required some experimenting with the supercharged versions to obtain the maximum benefits in acceleration without having the rear wheels spin. The experienced installers at Paxton's (who say 50 per cent of the blowers are currently going on T-Birds) advised making the gear changes from low to drive, with the Fordomatic, at 4700 rpm on the tachometer.

Slightly better times were recorded with the overdrive arrangement, except on the 0-45 mph times where time required for engaging the clutch and shifting gears reduced whatever benefits the system provided mechanically. The following are the best times in seconds obtained with each car:

SUPERCHARGED

	Fordomatic	Overdrive
0-30 mph	3	2.2
0-45 mph	5	5
0-60 mph	8	6.8

Comparison of these times with figures from three previously published reports on Thunderbird performance (all involving Fordomatic transmissions) provides interesting material for speculation:

UNSUPERCHARGED

	Test #1	Test #2	Test #3
0-30 mph	4	3.7	4.3
0-45 mph	—	—	—
0-60 mph	11	9.5	10.75

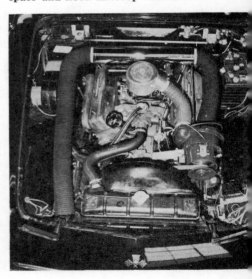

McCulloch supercharger installation on Thunderbird owned by Jane Russell of the movies. If the T-Bird gets fuel injection next year, as rumored, mounting the blower will be easier than ever, with underhood gains in space and hood airscoop will vanish.

The similarity of the extremely graceful Thunderbird to '55 Ford station wagons and sedans is apparent in above photo. Photo (right) emphasizes car's lowness.

Unique is the word for Ford's creation—a good car but neither fish nor flesh nor good red herring . . .

The Thunderbird

By G. M. LIGHTOWLER

IN PRESENTING the Thunderbird the Ford Motor Company has introduced a new type of automobile and offers, to individualist drivers, a model that is at present without parallel.

Before extolling its virtues and criticizing its faults, let it be said quite categorically that the Thunderbird is *not* a sports car and is not sold as such. The Ford Motor Company has been particularly careful in its advertising and publicity to point out that it is a "personalized car," designed for a distinctive group of motorists—the business executive. the country club habitue and the young man-about-town. It is strictly a two-seater for it is decidedly uncomfortable for three because of the high transmission hump and the position of the floor gear-shift lever. It is not a car for general family transportation; only as a second car and general runabout does it fit into the pattern of the family motorist. Those who have raced the Thunderbird (and there are quite a number) either on dirt tracks or road circuits. have done so purely as private ventures and without the approval of the manufacturer.

Much has already been written about the Thunderbird, but most of it from the wrong angle—the sports angle. In reviewing the Thunderbird we are going to deal with it from the point of view

Straight lines in body design and the pleasing lack of a mass of chrome add to sleek appearance of the Thunderbird.

of the discriminating driver who has no intention of competing in races or rallies, but who wishes to own a sporty-looking car that provides more driving enjoyment than the average sedan.

The Thunderbird is a graceful and attractive automobile. Its lines are straight and sure, its stance businesslike. The limited use of chrome is most pleasing and indicates the designer's clarity of thought—there is no fussiness about the exterior of the car. The relationship of the Thunderbird to other 1955 Ford models is apparent at first sight, and although the Ford Company tell us in their advertising that their sedans and station wagons are "Thunderbird-styled," one cannot but think that the lines of the Thunderbird were dictated by those of the conventional models rather than vice versa.

From a critical point of view, it might be considered that the car is too wide for its height. However, this width was probably predetermined by the decision to use certain components common to the regular '55 Fords. To keep the cost of the car within reasonable limits this use of existing plant equipment and components is commendable, and demonstrates the versatility

of the design department. Usually a car of this nature is constructed of specially designed parts throughout, the parts requiring special presses and machinery for their manufacture. If this procedure had been followed the cost of the car would have been so high that Thunderbirds would only be within reach of the wealthy.

The bulbous overriders on the front and rear bumpers could well be re-designed, for they do little to enhance the elegance of the car; this also applies to the air intake on top of the hood which could have been dealt with in a more delicate manner and probably moved forward. The use of standard braking and traffic signal-light fixtures in the rear seems out of place and again a smaller and more finely designed attachment would blend better.

A plastic top is available for those

Massiveness of top frame is evident in this picture. Erection of top is job, even for two; canvas catches easily.

Full power equipment

Under the hood is all motor, compact yet not cluttered. This is modified Mercury engine with 3.75-inch bore.

who like a coupe, and this accessory improves the look of what is already one of the most distinguished American-manufactured automobiles on the road today.

The color schemes for the Thunderbird are harmonious with the general design and the convertible we were loaned, through the courtesy of William A. Lashley, public relations manager of the Washington, D. C., office of the Ford Company, had a body finish of a pleasant duck-egg blue. with cockpit fittings in dark green, blue and white. The canvas top was black.

The car had full power equipment—power-operated four-way seats, power-operated windows, power brakes and Fordomatic transmission.

With the easily adjustable seat, covered in a washable plastic, and the adjustable steering wheel, the driver can find a position that is not only comfortable but one from which he can easily view all four fenders. The well defined line of the front fenders. viewed from an ideal height, make the job of aiming the car along a desired line similar to aiming a rifle, and after only a short period of familiarization the car can be positioned with remarkable accuracy.

We are still not happy about wrap-around windshields, despite the fact that we have driven only two 1955 cars

Photo by Swann Studio

Bulbous protrusions on bumpers do little to enhance grace of the car, while braking and traffic signal-light fixtures seem out of place on this type auto.

The Thunderbird we tested was beautifully finished in a pleasing duck-egg blue. Dark green was added to interior.

The gear-shift lever is admirably placed but CAR LIFE'S test driver found the brake pedal rather poorly positioned.

that have not been so equipped. The blind spot caused by the windshield post has not been eliminated, but moved back. This means that one has to move one's head considerably to see around it. Had the old curved shield been used, the amount of glass would have been reduced, the instrument panel could have been moved further forward, and driving in the dark or on a rainy day simplified. There is distortion in any curved surface of glass, this distortion increasing with the curvature. There is also difficulty in wiping a curved glass surface, the difficulty increasing with the amount of bend. Wraparound windshields may well be good selling points, but they do not contribute to good automobile operation.

The adoption of the wraparound and the rearward movement of the pillar has resulted in a most unfortunate protrusion into the doorway. This jutting angle, which is very low, definitely interferes with entry and exit from the driver's seat, especially when the seat is well forward and the steering wheel adjusted to lie in the driver's lap. The instrument panel of the car, very much 1955 Ford in appearance, is generally well laid out with all the knobs easily reached and all the instruments clearly visible. But the use of the conventional speedometer casing and attached dials is disappointing, particularly as a tachometer is installed as well as a clock with a large second sweep-hand. The speedometer might well be redesigned to better suit the character of the car.

In the driver's seat, one immediately gets the "feel" of the stubby gear-shift lever, which is admirably placed so that one's hand falls right on it. In the car we drove, fitted with automatic transmission, the lever was used merely for initial selection of the drive required, although there were several occasions when low gear had to be selected in a hurry and the car later put back into normal drive.

One of the bad features of the cockpit is the position of the brake, which demands excessive lifting of the foot from the accelerator and a definite placing of it on the brake pedal—that is, if conventional braking is used and the pedal is not operated by the left foot.

The erection and lowering of the canvas top is somewhat of a task and it is more advisable to tackle the job with some assistance. The frame work, geometrically of good design, is extremely heavy and can become bothersome to even two people. The cover tends to become caught in the top joints of the frame and it should be reinforced at the points of stress to avoid ripping.

When down, the top nestles neatly behind the seats and is covered with a plastic cover with press studs that hold it to the floor. Due to the flimsy nature

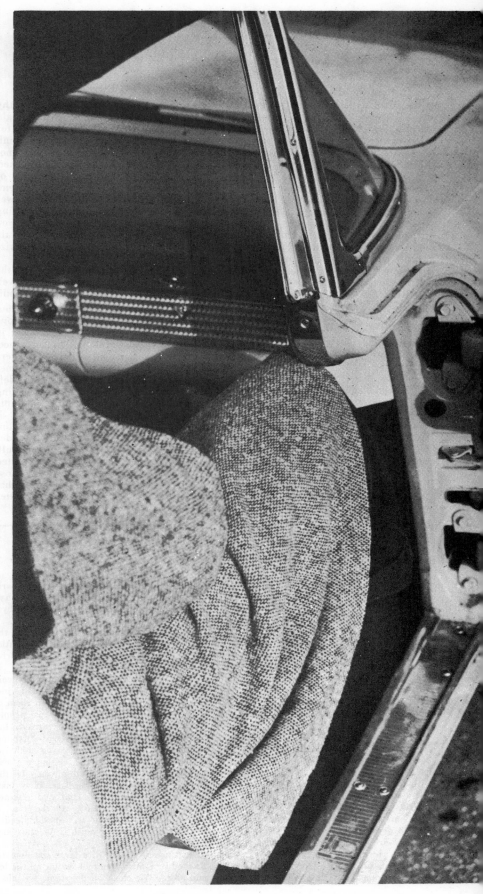

Backward movement of windshield pillar presents very disturbing jutting angle.

The Thunderbird

of the cover and the tug with which one has to remove this type of press stud, tearing is a definite danger unless great care is exercised—something likely to be overlooked when caught suddenly in a heavy rain and the top has to be raised in a hurry.

The trunk of the car is small by normal standards, although it is adequate for selected luggage for two persons for a two-week vacation. The position of the spare wheel in the trunk leaves one hoping that a puncture will not be encountered, for removing the spare must entail a great amount of twisting and heaving.

Driving the Thunderbird is no exacting procedure and becomes, after a short period at the wheel, a very enjoyable pastime. What will impress the driver as soon as he touches the accelerator is the fantastic pick-up and the car's extreme light feeling. Power-steering, of which we don't generally approve on high-powered automobiles, may take a little getting used to, but once its sensitivity has been appreciated and remembered for the emergency swing of the wheel, confidence will be gained.

The power-operated brakes are fierce and if not treated with respect can cause some embarrassing moments, particularly if the road surface is wet or slick. It was not possible to put the car through a vigorous braking test over a lengthy period, but judging from recorded high-speed performance of Thunderbirds for hours on end, we are inclined to think that brake fade is prevalent, though not enough to trouble the average owner.

Top speed of the car is in excess of 100 mph.—far too fast to be contemplated by the average driver, yet power enough for any emergency. Cruising speed is in the seventies—provided you reside, or are passing through, a state that is broadminded enough to authorize such a speed.

The handling characteristics of the car can be a little worrying when traveling at speed. Being such a low-built automobile (50.2 inches high without top and 5.5-inch ground clearance), one is inclined to expect the ultimate in cornering and braking performance. Such, however, is not the case. There is a decided lean on taking any corner at maximum speeds; there is considerable knee-bending on violent braking (suspension is decidedly soft). Attempts to make the rear-end break away at reasonable speeds met with failure, but the promotion of a four-wheel drift under favorable conditions was not too difficult. These conditions may well be attributed to the fitting of low-pressure tires, whose squeal at times gives the impression that speed and opposing forces are greater than they actually are.

No accurate figures were taken on gas mileage, but mixing heavy-footed driving on the country road with careful motoring and much city crossing (when congestion was at its worst), a figure of 16 miles to the gallon seemed commendable. During all the time we drove the car, our tendency to accelerate hard was not curbed and with a little care gas economy could be greatly increased. as is the case with most automobiles.

The power unit for the Thunderbird is a modified Mercury engine with a displacement of 292 cubic inches (4786 cc.) and a bore and stroke of 3.75x3.30 inches, utilizing a compression ratio of 8.1:1 with normal transmission and 8.5:1 with automatic.

The engine compartment is compact and clean in arrangement—it is full of machinery, but all units are easily accessible for service. The hood opens from the rear, being hinged forward of the radiator.

Summarizing, the Thunderbird is lots of fun. It is neither fish nor flesh nor good red herring for comparison purposes, being neither a true sports car nor a conventional automobile. It might be called the successful child of an industry that is forced to abide by dictates that it itself created. It is as American as the game of baseball. ☆☆

THUNDERBIRD . . .
Continued from page 9

No data is available on the suspension characteristics other than the statement that the car has passenger car comfort with "firm springs for stability and security".

The brakes are Bendix duo-servo types with 11-inch drums. Front linings are 2 inches wide, rear linings are 1.75 inches. A vacuum booster is optional at extra cost. Wheels and tires are specially designed to withstand continuous high-speed driving and the Thunderbird becomes the first American car to use tubeless tires as standard equipment.

Reverting back to the powerplant, the new 292 cu in. Y-block V-8 has .125 inch more bore, .200 more stroke than the 1954 Mercury. The carburetor has 4 barrels supplied with cool air through a hood bulge that is not a dummy. Exhaust system is dual with reverse-flow mufflers. The clutch is 11 inches in diameter and of the conventional sdp (single dry plate) type.

There are 3 transmission options: conventional 3 speed, conventional with overdrive, or Fordomatic. For the Zephyr-gear enthusiast, 1st speed has the same ratio as the 06H model L-Z (2.33:1), 2nd speed is nearly the same as the 26H Lincoln Zephyr (1.48:1). Control of all transmissions is by a very neat floor-mounted lever.

The rear axle housing is similar to the Spicer-type, with hypoid gears. Axle ratios are 3.73 with 3-speeds, 3.92 with overdrive and 3.31 with Fordomatic.

Body construction is all-steel with convertible-type windows and wrap-around windshield. The single seat provides hip room of 60.2 inches, but is designed for two people. A middle passenger can be carried, but cushion depth over the propeller-shaft tunnel is restricted. The top is black rayon cloth and folds to a protected position behind the seat. An optional hard-top, weighing only 65 lbs. is available, made of fiberglass. It is insulated against sound and heat and retained by 4 toggle-action clamps at the rear, 2 similar clamps on the windshield header. The fiberglass top is finished in the same color as the car.

Instruments consist of a large speedometer flanked by a 5000 rpm tachometer on the left and an electric clock on the right. The clock has a sweep-second hand and matches the tach. Fuel and temperature gauges complete the instrumentation, with warning lights for no-charge and low oil pressure.

Upholstery is all-vinyl in white with trim to match the body color. Color choice will be black, torch red or turquoise. No price has been announced, but it is expected to be under $4000. ●

SPECIFICATIONS

Wheelbase, in.	102
Tread, front	56
rear	56
Tire size	6.70-15
Curb weight, lbs.	3147
distribution	52/48
Engine	ohv V-8
Bore and stroke	3.75 x 3.30
Displacement, cu in.	292
	(4787 cc)
Bhp	not available
Gear ratios (oa. - std. trans.)	
high	3.73
2nd	5.52
1st.	8.69

Classic Motorbooks ™

729 PROSPECT AVENUE
OSCEOLA, WI 54020, U.S.A. • 1-800-826-6600

ORDER NUMBER	314578-000
CUSTOMER NUMBER	283726
DATE	6/27/94

SOLD
TO RUSSELL HAWORTH

1405 W ORCHARD LN
CARLSBAD   NM   88220-0000

LOCATION	ITEM NUMBER	QUANTITY	DESCRIPTION	PRICE	STATUS
04-A1	105032	1	TBRD 55-57	16.95	

MERCHANDISE	SHIPPING/HANDLING	STATE TAX	TOTAL AMOUNT	AMOUNT PAID	BALANCE DUE	CREDIT
16.95	4.50	.85	22.30	22.30		

SHIP VIA: RP

339309001

THANK YOU FOR YOUR ORDER. WE LOOK FORWARD TO
SERVING YOU AGAIN IN THE FUTURE. IF WE CAN BE OF
SERVICE TO YOU, PLEASE CALL US ON OUR TOLL FREE
HOT LINE - 1-800-826-6600.

MASTER CHARGE

339309001

SEE REVERSE SIDE FOR RETURN AND REORDER INFORMATION AND **STATUS** OF UNSHIPPED MERCHANDISE

STFW
****** WI 1

Classic Motorbooks ™

729 PROSPECT AVENUE • OSCEOLA, WI 54020, U.S.A.

FORWARDING AND RETURN POSTAGE GUARANTEED

DATE
6/27/94

ORDER #
314578-000

SHIP VIA
RP DAG 017

PRESORT SPEC 4TH CLASS
U.S. POSTAGE PAID
OSCEOLA, WISCONSIN
PERMIT NO. 32

PKGID   339309003

TO RUSSELL HAWORTH
1405 W ORCHARD LN
CARLSBAD   NM 88220-0000

339309003

Classic Motorbooks ™

729 PROSPECT AVENUE • OSCEOLA, WI 54020, U.S.A.

FORWARDING AND RETURN POSTAGE GUARANTEED

DATE
6/27/94

ORDER #
314578-000

SHIP VIA
RP DAG 017

PRESORT SPEC 4TH CLASS
U.S. POSTAGE PAID
OSCEOLA, WISCONSIN
PERMIT NO. 32

PKGID   339309004

TO RUSSELL HAWORTH
1405 W ORCHARD LN
CARLSBAD   NM 88220-0000

S T A T U S

STATUS OF UNSHIPPED MERCHANDISE

TOS — Temporarily Out of Stock-expect
to ship within 30 days

NPO — New Publication on Order-will
ship when initial stock is received

OP — Out of Print-no longer being printed
NA — No longer Available from us
OSI — Out of Stock Indefinitely-may be
available in 6-12 months-Please reorder

CREDIT CARD CUSTOMERS — You have been charged only for items shipped plus postage & handling
and sales tax where applicable.

R E T U R N S

If for any reason you are not completely satisfied with your purchase, return it **within 14 days**
of receipt for replacement, exchange or refund.

1. Complete information below and return with package.
2. Address your package with return label provided below.
3. For your protection we suggest you return items via UPS or Insured Parcel Post.

Qty	Item #	Description	Desired Action	Reason Code	Unit Price	Total Credit

DESIRED ACTION

1. Please replace
2. Reorder different and/or additional merchandise
3. Please refund by original method of payment

REASON CODE — Please Explain Below

1. Received damaged/defective
2. Received incorrect merchandise
3. Merchandise on back-order too long
4. Unsatisfactory service
5. Other

R E O R D E R

If Desired Action is option 1 or 2 above please complete below:

Qty	Item #	Description	Price	Total	Ship to: If Different
					Name
					Address
					City
					State Zip Code

☐ Check or Money order enclosed
☐ Visa   ☐ American Express
☐ Mastercard   ☐ Discover
Card #_____
Expiration date_____
Signature_____

Please indicate form of payment for any amount due.

*Residents of CA, CT, D.C., HI, IL, KS, MA, MN, NE, NM, NV & WI please add your state sales tax.

Return explanation and customer
concerns suggestions or comments.

_____
_____
_____
_____

Use this label to return merchandise. Fasten with cellophane tape.

FROM

_____
_____
_____
_____

TO

Classic Motorbooks T.M.

729 PROSPECT AVENUE
OSCEOLA, WI 54020, U.S.A.

THE THUNDERBIRD

Continued from Page 46

deviated from the norm that has been wholeheartedly accepted by the postwar public. According to authoritative figures, at the end of 1954, a bare two-and-a-half months after its introduction, it had already sold more copies than its competitors with their considerably longer life spans. To date, about nine months since it hit the showrooms, roughly 11,000 T-Birds have been delivered, and in spite of a 65 car per day production rate, the supply is two-and-a-half months behind the demand.

The Thunderbird project began in 1949, the same year a few U.S. motorists discovered MG's. FMC's Product Planning department noted that a sports car boom seemed to be in the making. It's the business of Product Planning to predict what the public will be ready for in the years ahead, and they called the shot—a sports machine, but one suited to American requirements. There was another angle, too, one that seemed to fit in perfectly. The statistical experts discovered that in addition to the mounting interest in sports cars, a steadily increasing number of U.S. families owned two or more cars. So Market Research recommended that the company build a new kind of automobile that would have equally strong appeal in both the expanding sports car and "second-car" markets. Top brass OK'd the recommendation and passed it on to the Product Planning division, as follows:

1. The car must have really brilliant performance, good enough to permit it to hold its own in racing, although this would be a bonus feature and not a main objective. It must be able to out-perform anything an owner would be likely to meet on street or highway, including expensive foreign high-performance cars.

2. Cornering and handling qualities must closely approach those of all-out sports cars. The ride must be flat and firm, firmer than in standard U.S. passenger car practice, but not harsh.

3. The car had to be styled as a prestige vehicle, reflecting the best of good taste. It would have to look fleet and graceful, but at the same time avoid the clichés of European styling. Intended to appeal to the American mass market, it must have a purely American look.

4. Every aspect of passenger comfort and convenience had to be provided for. This would include a choice of manual-shift, OD, or automatic transmission and the availability of the whole range of power-assist devices. All-weather protection, leg room, hip room, head room, luggage space had to be up to accepted U.S. standards.

FMC executives tell me that all this planning took place in 1949 and early 1950, when stylists and engineers went to work figuring out the car's package size. Good handling qualities demanded a short wheelbase, and they selected one of 102 inches. A high performance car demands

a stiff frame, so they used a shortened version of the rugged Ford-convertible "X" frame. For good handling a car also has to have approximately equal distribution of weight between the front and the rear wheels, so the engineers put the engine a few inches farther aft in the frame than is the case in standard practice. The Bird's engine fan is about flush with the front wheel hubs.

Everyone agreed that a low profile would give the car dash and class. To get it, the engineers brought the hood down around the carburetor air cleaner.

Another problem the low profile posed, along with the farther-back engine location, was getting plenty of leg room for the passengers. This was solved by seating riders well back on the chassis. The arrangement left plenty of room for luggage space, but no room for the usual convertible top that can be stacked in a space-wasting horizontal recess. So the Bird has a top that stows vertically in a narrow recess behind the seat-back.

These details, and hundreds of others like them, were worked out by a couple of hundred technicians and engineers over a period of years. First, they'd lay a detail out on paper. Then they'd try it out on a wooden "body buck" big enough for the designers to get in and out of. After a whole series of body bucks had been evolved, approximations of the final Bird were cobbled from wood, clay and metal. Then a few actual prototypes were hand-built. And, at last, the dimensions and other specifications of the final Thunderbird were arrived at.

Almost exactly six years passed from the time Market Research turned its attention to sports car until Ford's "personal" car was introduced. The thousands of creative man-hours that were put into the project have been amply paid for by the public's solid acceptance of the car. It isn't only the performance-minded "average" driver that craves the T-Bird. Last year Juan Manuel Fangio, world's champion of Grand Prix racing, told me that he considered the Thunderbird one of the most ideal automobiles built anywhere in the world—and he was panting to get one. He backed up his statement a few weeks later by buying a Bird. It takes a mighty versatile car to have as much appeal for a seasoned racing professional as it does for a housewife.

It is this sweeping acceptance of the Thunderbird that proves that it comes closest to being the American car that enthusiasts have demanded so loudly and so long. The Thunderbird successfully and obviously satisfies a need of American motorists, and is an inspired piece of shrewd and calculated planning.

The Thunderbird is the first of the new U. S. *luxury* cars, the pioneer, and a milestone in the postwar progress of the automobile. Watch its influence closely. It's the first of "tomorrow's" cars. ●

CONTINUED FROM PAGE 92
Taking the Hawk over the same course we used for the Corvette and Thunderbird, I was disappointed in the way it handled. The supercharged power was lost in tight turns, since I was forced to get off the throttle in order to get the front end under control. The body leaned considerably through the turns, and the wheel felt sluggish in my hands. Recovery was not as rapid as I would have liked it, which meant taking the turns considerably slower than I did with the other cars.

Despite all this, however, the '57 Hawk is an improvement over the '56. Studebaker engineers have done much to eliminate the handling problem by lightening the front end and adding the new variable-ratio steering that works through a gear arrangement. This is quite an improvement over last year's car.

Then, too, Studebaker's new "Twin Traction" delivers engine power to the "gripping" wheel on slippery streets (or to the inside wheel on turns), giving the Hawk more roadability than before. The Twin-Traction differential is optional at extra cost.

Studebaker craftsmanship has been something to boast about for years, and this fact is evident in the workmanship on the '57 Golden Hawk. I noticed this especially with the brakes—best of the three cars tested. I had very little brake fade, except on the panic stop at 100 mph. The quick stop was smooth despite our speed, and while there was a certain amount of fade the recovery was exceptionally rapid.

Finned drums, which shed heat by allowing cool air to circulate around the lining, was the answer here. After the panic stop I noticed some fade; but it was gone by the time I turned the car around and tried the brakes again.

Summing it up, I believe all three cars are a credit to American stliying and engineering. I cannot recommend one over the other because public acceptance depends on individual likes and needs. The Corvette has done well toward capturing the true sports-car enthusiast. The Thunderbird ranks as an "in-betweener", with an appealing emphasis on both the sports-car angle and passenger-car comfort. The Golden Hawk, by the same token has a big bill to fill by appealing to family needs as well as sports enthusiasts.

In all three cases, I feel that these three cars have a definite place in American motoring. They give evidence of America's successful venture into sports car styling; a venture that, only a few years ago, was surrounded by skepticism. But it has gone on with constant improvements that promise an even greater future. ●

AFTER THE GIRLS, THE JOURNALISTS: After the pictures had been taken, the car was handed over to us for some driving around Albert Park, Melbourne.

A COUPLE of weeks ago I drove the most exciting car to come my way for many a long day —Ford's Thunderbird.

It's a car not seen in Australia. Made in America and sold in numbers there, and presumably wherever people pay in dollars, it combines the comfort and style features of the big U.S. car with some of the features of a sports car.

Ford are careful NOT to call it a sports car, although naturally most buyers do. Ford calls it a "personal car".

Recently, though, Ford brought a Thunderbird to Australia for display purposes. And at a press gathering in Melbourne, we were given the opportunity to try it out for ourselves.

Believe me, this car has really got thunder. Its engine develops 193 S.A.E. horsepower at 4,400 r.p.m., which in brake horsepower,

Left: This picture gives you an idea of the driver's vision. The round dials on either side of the speedometer are the rev. counter and clock.

The lines of the Thunderbird are really smooth (below). Note the wind-up windows. Currency restrictions prevent Australian buyers driving them. In any case, the out-of-wack dollar exchange rate would push their price over £2,000.

...ird has THUNDER

...respondent tried out the Ford Thunderbird
... and is very impressed.

By Phil Goldin

Upholstery on this car was red and white. A good point is are wide-opening doors. Vision from the wrap-around screen is embracing.

Massive engine displaces 4¾ litres. Notice accessible dip stick, distributor, coil. Bonnet opens forward, is hinged at front.

I guess, would be nudging 170. The result in a car weighing 27¾ cwt. is a lot of heft.

The pictures will show you that the car is quite large. It has a single bench seat which will seat three, and a big luggage locker. From bumper to bumper it measures 14 ft. 7 in., and it's a couple of inches short of six feet wide. That door is only 3 ft. 10 in. from the ground, too.

The 193 horsepower comes from a 4.8 litre, o.h.v. V-8 engine. The torque — which gives acceleration and climbing — is a whopping 280 lb. ft. Compression is 8.1 to 1.

The Thunderbird I drove had a standard three-speed gearbox with a floor-mounted shift lever. Buyers in America can have automatic transmission and power brakes if they wish. Not having tried one with automatic gear changing, I don't know what it would be like. I know, though, that the ordinary gearbox is smooth and positive.

The seating position can be adjusted to any driver's needs. A touch on a button and the electric seat adjustment motor raises or lowers the cushion. It moves it forward and back as well.

The steering wheel is adjustable for reach, a feature lacking in most cars today.

The finish and fittings are of a craftsman standard. A glance at the pictures will show what I mean.

On the road there is a feeling of tremendous power. This car wasn't properly run in, so high speeds in the gears weren't possible.

To give you an idea of what the power is like, we came up behind another car which was doing 30.

We sat behind him for a moment, then pulled out to pass. We passed his rear bumper at 38. We pulled in a bare length ahead of him doing 60.

At 60, to use an old expression, there seems to be another 60 m.p.h. to come. The Ford man told me that the top speed of the car is in the vicinity of 120 m.p.h.

Comfort is good. The suspension wafts the car over the road gutter, on to rough ground, with no jolting and bouncing of the passengers.

Handling seems good as well. As one takes it in to a tightening turn there is only slight tyre squeal, and there is a comforting road-hugging feel.

Braking was good, although we couldn't test for things like fade. But in a panic stop from 30, there is no side pull or disconcerting effects.

It is manoeuvrable, and with a turning circle of 36 feet, deals with most streets in one bite.

Flexibility? Well, we slowed to a silky crawl at about 5 m.p.h. — and then took off with whiplash go.

Of course, you don't have to flatten the Bird in every gear

everywhere. In fact, of its virtues its silence, flexibility in top gear and effortless driving are among the highest.

Criticisms? Well, I thought the steering wheel was a little small, but I'm used to a big wheel. I found the foot pedals too small and cramping as well.

One impression stayed with me. It was that American engineers, in this case from Ford, are no slouches at design and styling. And their production engineers and sales staff put this car into the hands of the buyer for as many man hours as we would have to work to buy even the smallest of small runabouts.

When I got home I looked up the results of an independent test of a Bird in America. Top speed was 112 m.p.h. At 5,000 r.p.m., the car did 82 m.p.h. in second and 50 m.p.h. in first.

A standing quarter mile went under the wheels in — hold your hat — 16.9 seconds. As comparison, a well-tuned Holden will reel it off in 21 seconds and an M.G. about the same.

Petrol consumption was 15 m.p.g. driven hard, 18 m.p.g. cruised at around 60 to 70 . . . and the U.S. gallon is a fifth smaller than ours.

However, the speedometer was very optomistic — it read 100 at a genuine 90. Which, says the tester, may account for the starry-eyed stories of owners who get 130 m.p.h.!

Frontal appearance of '56 T-Bird is unchanged from 1955. New are controversial rear-mounted spare, hardtop with port holes in sides.

DRIVER'S REPORT—
THE 1956 THUNDERBIRD

BY KEN FERMOYLE

How does the new T-Bird go? It's hotter, naturally—and there are other changes upon which opinion is divided

IT'S BEEN a lot of years since an automobile caught the public fancy as quickly and completely as the Ford Thunderbird. Will the 1956 version be able to keep the trend going?

The new T-Bird is basically unchanged from the original 1955 model. Of the changes that were made, some are for the better—others might better have been skipped.

One of the things that caused the '55 to go was the way the car went! It was a hot car and the new one is even more so. Horsepower is up across the board and it shows up in performance.

Two Thunderbirds were used for this report both Ford-o-Matic jobs with the 312-cubic-inch V-8 rated at 225 hp. They averaged nine seconds flat in a number of 0 to 60 mph runs, with several being timed a couple of tenths of a second faster.

(Neither of the T-Birds tested, incidentally, had been given any special tuning and were comparable to one an average customer might get off the showroom floor.)

Times for 0 to 30 mph checks averaged out to just about 3.5 seconds and the 'Birds got from 50 to 80 mph in 10 seconds. Unfortunately, traffic and weather conditions prevented adequate top speed checks. It was a rare 'Bird that couldn't turn between 115 and 120 mph in 1955; automatic shift models generally averaged about 118 and the overdrive jobs were good for 120 or a shade better. It's reasonable to expect the 1956 models to do a bit faster than this.

It may be that the 1956 won't top last year's model in the top speed department, however, due to one of the more important changes made in the car. Offsetting the increased power is that conti-

---

What a T-Bird owner thinks

AS THE OWNER of a 1956 Thunderbird, equipped with a manual shift transmission, I was eager to drive one of the Ford-O-Matic test report cars to see for myself exactly what differences there were between the two types.

The mechanical differences, other than the transmissions, consist of 312 cubic inches and a 9-to-1 compression ratio, plus a 3.31-to-1 rear axle ratio in the automatic box 'Bird; and 292 inches at 8.4-to-1 and a 3.73-to-1 ring and pinion in the manual shift version.

Driving the 'Bird-O-Matic gave me a completely unrelated feeling to the sensations obtained in my own car. In fact, it was almost like another machine. There was the same exhilarating forward thrust when the throttle was slammed home and the effect was retained throughout the driving range. Most evident, however, was the lack of positive engagement in the torque-converter

when a conscious effort was made to give it the works.

Shifting from low range to drive can be touchy. Lack of friction makes it too easy to bypass drive and go on to neutral. On a proper shift change, however, the rear tires bawl and the torque goes to work with the pinion trying to climb the ring gear and wrap the rear springs around the axle housings. A definitely mushy sensation accompanies this ratio change and a time lag occurs before forward acceleration really begins.

Absence of direct connection, as in the three-speed unit, is the reason for the equalizing extra 23 ponies in the 'matic, and they do the job as far as seat-of-the-pants driving goes. An intense interest is created in those of us who are do-it-yourself shifters as to the performance possibilities of our Thunderbirds should they, too, be equipped with the 225-hp engine.—*Lynn Wineland.*

Early 1956 'Birds had only two mufflers, causing resonance inside car. Switch to quad muffler system solved problem.

Fewer right angle bends in tail pipe cut back pressure as compared to '55 system. Exhaust is partially deflected by bumper.

Power seat, window controls are set in left front door panel where they are easily accessible. The side vents are new.

nental tire mounted at the rear. Such a set-up adds a lot of drag at the high end of the speed range and can easily cut several miles off top speed.

The continental mounting is one of the most controversial features added to the 1956 T-Bird. It was added to get the spare out of the luggage compartment and increase carrying capacity. Ford reports that inadequate luggage space was one of the features the car was criticized for in 1955. Removing the tire adds some 20 per cent to the usable area in the trunk.

Personally I feel it might have been better to make the continental kit an option. It not only creates more wind resistance but I think it detracts from the car's appearance. Quite a few people have agreed with me so far.

Having the spare mounted at the extreme rear of the car does seem to result in a bit better weight distribution, however. The ratio in 1955 was about 52 per cent front, 48 per cent rear. Although I wasn't able to check it on scales, the outside spare may help bring this closer to 50-50. My impression was that traction is slightly improved.

Other than that, handling of the '56 is not much different from the '55. A few minor changes were made to the suspension—longer rear springs, revalved shocks —to give a flatter ride. This has resulted in a slight improvement in the new T-Bird's cornering potential, but the 1955 model was so good in this department that it's difficult to assess the benefit of the changes.

The ride is firm by passenger car standards, outrageously comfortable when compared to most sport cars. The T-Bird sticks to the road well, doesn't bounce badly or take off into space after hitting humps. You feel irregularities in road surfaces more than you would in your family sedan but not enough to shake you up to any degree. In return, you get a degree of control and maneuverability that approaches sport car standards.

Unfortunately, Ford has slowed up the

Continental tire mounting must be swung back out of way to permit access to gas filler pipe on the 1956 T-Bird.

Like predecessors, new T-Bird has an adjustable steering wheel. Turning of a knurled collar locks wheel in position.

steering on the new T-Birds. The ratio has been upped from 20 to 23-to-1 and 4¾ turns are required to go from lock to lock. This is hard to understand, since anyone who feels the steering is too stiff can get power steering. In fact, most 1955 models were sold with this option. At any rate, the slow steering definitely hurts the otherwise excellent high speed maneuvering potential of the car.

A real improvement is the optional fiber-glass top with side portholes. These openings, though not very large, do permit better visibility to the sides and are a boon in traffic and tight quarters. Besides, I think they look good. They seem to fit in well with the T-Bird's jaunty appearance. If you disagree, the top with blind rear quarters which was offered last year is still available.

The 312-inch engine offered with Ford-o-Matic is basically the same as the current Mercury power plant. Compression ratio is 9-to-1 and its 225 horses are delivered at 4600 rpm. An engine of the same size is used in overdrive T-Birds, but it has lower compression ratio, 8.4-to-1, and is rated at 215 horsepower. Torque is 324 foot pounds for the hotter engine, 317 for the latter—peak torque coming in at 2600 rpm for both.

A smaller 292-cubic-inch engine with 8.4-to-1 compression ratio is offered for standard shift T-Birds. This is similar to the one offered on all 1955 models but horsepower has been increased to 202 (from either 193 or 198 last year, depending on transmission). The boost is due mainly to higher valve lift; valve timing hasn't been altered.

Hydraulic valve lifters are not used in any of the three engines. As in all other 1956 Ford products a 12-volt electrical system is used instead of the 6-volt.

Ford calls the T-Bird a "personal car," not a sport car. And it isn't a sport car in the sense that a purist uses the term. It certainly is a lot of fun to drive, however. I'll be very much surprised if the new model doesn't meet with the same success the 1955 did. •

PERFORMANCE ☑ ☑ ☑ ☑ ☐

Equals all stock cars and is exceeded only by the Studebaker Golden Hawk. Will accelerate from 0 to 60 mph in 10 seconds and reach an honest 110 mph.

STYLING ☑ ☑ ☑ ☑ ☑

Crisp and functional, especially with the fibreglass hardtop which lends the car a family resemblance to the Continental Mark II. A welcome change from the smeared-with-chrome look of conventional passenger cars.

RIDING COMFORT ☑ ☑ ☑ ☑ ☐

The T-Bird must be firmly suspended, but Ford engineers have managed to build in a remarkably smooth ride equal to many family sedans. On good roads the T-Bird is more restful than ordinary cars because of the *complete* absence of rolling, swaying and pitching.

INTERIOR DESIGN ☑ ☑ ☑ ☑ ☑

Has more room, better forward vision and greater ease of entrance and exit than others of its type. The solid rear quarter of both the hard and soft tops creates a blind spot that is sometimes annoying when maneuvering in thick traffic.

ROADABILITY ☑ ☑ ☑ ☑ ☐

The T-Bird, along with Corvette, surpasses every other production car built. It has amazing staying power when cornering and responds well to correction when the rear end can be forced into a slide. At speeds of 95 and up car loses some of its hold on the road and is prone to wander and drift even on slight curves.

EASE OF CONTROL ☑ ☑ ☑ ☑ ☐

Power steering is not really essential. "Slow" (20 to 1) steering detracts from instant response to road conditions. Brakes work effectively for straight stops in decelerating below 80 mph. Above that speed car has a tendency to slow to left or right when brakes are hit.

ECONOMY ☑ ☑ ☑ ☐ ☐

A light foot will pay dividends, of course, but the T-Bird's acceleration potential will be hard for most owners to resist and the resulting gasoline mileage goes down accordingly.

SERVICEABILITY ☑ ☑ ☑ ☐ ☐

It's another case of a relatively large engine in a small cramped compartment. Top of engine components are easy to reach but spark plugs can only be reached from beneath the car.

WORKMANSHIP ☑ ☑ ☑ ☑ ☐

Standards of craftsmanship are generally high throughout the car with the glaring exception of the "folding" fabric top. On test car this top neither fitted in place in "up" position nor would it fold compactly behind the seat when folded down.

DURABILITY ☑ ☑ ☑ ☑ ☐

The T-Bird gives all evidence of being built for long life. Fordomatic Transmission on some '55 T-Birds downshifts a bit abruptly after several thousand miles, but this condition did not prevail on test '56 car.

VALUE PER DOLLAR ☑ ☑ ☑ ☑ ☐

The sales record of the T-Bird in its first full year of manufacture indicates a continuing demand. Car is well-designed and uses standard parts. It's a good buy for both long term useage or early resale.

1956

Specifications

Model	Ford Thunderbird
Wheelbase	102.0"
Length	185.0"
Engine Displacement	312 cu. in.
Bore and Stroke	3.80 by 3.44
Compression Ratio	9.0:1
Brake Horsepower	225
Torque	324 ft. lbs. at 2600
Electrical System	12 volt
Factory price, without accessories	$3102

FORD'S highly successful Thunderbird is little changed for 1956. Minor changes have boosted engine horsepower from 202 (with Fordomatic) to 225. Structurally, the only change is the addition of a built-in continental tire mounting.

There's an excellent reason for all the commotion about the spare tire. In last year's model it took a sizeable bite out of the rather limited trunk space. With the tire housed inside, only one man-sized suitcase could be fitted beside the tire with a few odds and ends tucked above and in front of it. Now, however, the spare snuggles in low and close to the body with the bumper neatly curved around it.

First and foremost the Thunderbird is not a true sports car.

Although it can go much faster than an MG, run dead heats with unmodified Austin-Healeys or Triumph TR-2s at speed and whip a Mercedes 190 SL in acceleration, the T-Bird still doesn't qualify and the others do.

However, to the Ford Motor Company's eternal credit, the T-Bird is not claimed a sports car . . . rather the maker calls it a "personal" car. Perhaps Ford is too modest because the T-Bird is (along with its U.S. rival, the Corvette) far closer to a real sports machine than any other production automobile built on this side of the Atlantic.

What the T-Bird offers the sporting motorist is a happy compromise that combines all the sports car characteristics that any unschooled driver needs on roads, streets and turnpikes, *plus* a host of comforts and conveniences afforded by

ANALYSIS:

thunderbird

FORD THUNDERBIRD

no true sports machine selling at two or three times the T-Bird's price.

In addition, the T-Bird is powered by a docile and readily-serviced "stock" engine that presents no mystery at all to any mechanic capable of adjusting a four-barrel carburetor and timing a modern V8.

The T-Bird's power-plant is capable of plodding back and forth to the station and the supermarket for months and then, with no more tuning than checking the oil and water, zooming up to 105 or 110 on the nearest unpoliced turnpike. Furthermore Ford engineers packaged all the T-Bird's performance and versatility in a body that is exceptionally comfortable and reasonably practical within obvious limitations of size.

Almost any man or woman driver can pilot a T-Bird from coast to coast in any season with as much comfort—and more safety—than in a luxury sedan. The level of comfort in the "personal" T-Bird has been kept very close to the conventional car; i.e., Ford's excellent fresh air heating and defrosting system, roll-up (or even power) windows and power operated seat.

For those motorists who have foregone clutch pushing in their conventional cars, the T-Bird is available with Fordomatic Transmission.

At speeds up to 85 the T-Bird seems completely the master of the road. An attentive driver feels just as relaxed as he might in a conventional sedan traveling 20 or 25 mph slower. At normal cruising speeds the T-Bird is as agile and

sure-footed as a polo pony and almost as maneuverable.

Adding to the driver's (and passenger's) comfort and piece of mind is just about the best forward vision available on any car. Despite the low top, the windshield sweeps so far back that it provides an excellent view of overhead signs and traffic lights.

Seating positions (power adjusted) are comfortable, and there's ample legroom. The seat, which although not as deeply padded as in a conventional sedan, provides adequate support at the thighs and small of the back. Incidentally, it is not physically impossible to add a third person in the middle of the T-Bird's seat, providing both the trip and the extra passenger's legs are short.

Instrumentation is generally good with Ford's big bubble-type speedometer and adjoining tachometer. An old-fashioned oil pressure gauge would be preferable to the, red warning light.

The quickly-removable fibreglass top is sturdy and really rattle-free. With windows buttoned up there was absolutely no trace of draft at high speed. Although the plastic convertible top can be "whisked into place" according to the Ford advertisement we recently read, the test car defeated the efforts of two adults (male) who labored some twenty minutes before giving up.

Summing up: A really excellent, well-balanced road car capable of sustained speeds much higher than most laws allow, and providing near true sports car roadability plus complete comfort for two passengers. ●

SCI tests the 1956 Ford Thunderbird

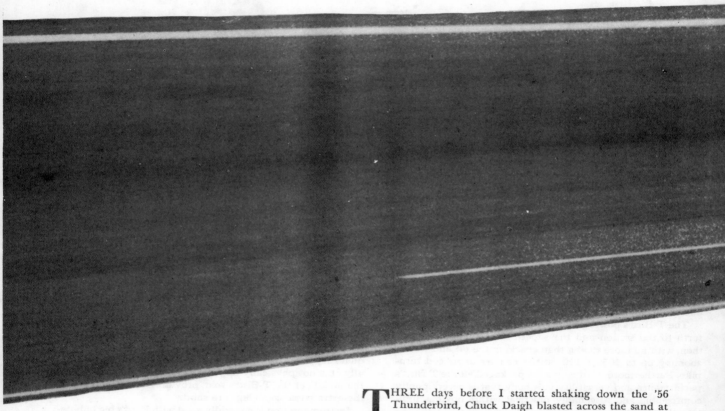

At kingman Arizona proving ground T-Bird laps test course with test driver J. B. Corbin behind wheel.

THREE days before I started shaking down the '56 Thunderbird, Chuck Daigh blasted across the sand at Daytona in a similar but souped car and covered the standing mile in 39.07 seconds, an average of over 92 mph for the distance. A few days later I clocked a stock T-Bird on Ford's Arizona proving ground at a sizzling 119 mph.

On the surface these figures seem to indicate that the T-Bird has a solid potential as a competition sports car, and that Ford has started to tap it. But it only looks that way when you take the figures out of the overall T-Bird context.

The Bird has plenty of brute strength but it is no sports car. Even though it corners very well this year, its chassis, steering and brakes still make it best suited to turnpikes and drag strips. Nevertheless, Bird sales in '55 wrote one of the big success stories of the year; 16,155 of them were sold, a new record for sports-type cars in the U. S. and far more than anyone at Ford expected. For '56, plant facilities have

*"As a touring car
and a sports car...
...an improvement
on its predecessor."*

been expanded to fill an expected 20,000 orders. This estimate, too, may be conservative.

Don't assume, though, that the screaming success of a not-quite-sports car means that the U. S. public is too dull and insensitive to know what it's buying. This is not true. Because if the Bird is something less than a sports car, it is something more, too. While it has only some of the handling and performance characteristics of full-fledged high-performance cars, it also has the comfort, convenience and luxury of good Detroit touring iron — qualities that most American drivers find it hard to do without.

As both a touring car and a sports car the '56·Bird is an improvement on its predecessor. But for as long as the car's sports side is going to be molded to fit the requirements of its touring side, there's bound to be a pretty tight limit on how good it can get from the point of view of the *pur sang* enthusiast. Last year it seemed possible that the Bird was the first of a series of transition cars that would lead to a mature sports machine. But this year all the indications are that the Bird is going to stay split down the middle and as schizoid as Dr. Jekyll.

You can't drive the car for 10 minutes without becoming aware of the contradictions and compromises that the car's double personality makes necessary. When you punch the throttle, for example, there's a pronounced lag before the car moves forward. This is the result of the use of a simple Hotchkiss drive — part of the Bird's touring car heritage — in combination with rear springs which are not at all firm enough to give good resistance to rear axle torque. Last year's car had 48-inch five-leaf half-elliptic rear springs and a ride that was definitely firmer than the Detroit standard. The new model has four-leaf springs at the rear and they are now 56 inches long. Now the car has as smooth and gentle a ride as most Detroit touring cars, and its roadability has not been adversely affected, but there is the lag. Furthermore, if you rock the steering wheel while you're going down a straight stretch, the car wallows heavily back and forth on its springs — the opposite of an all-of-a-piece feel. The sprung part of the car leads a life of its own, with little regard for the unsprung part.

The Bird's steering is another case in point. Last year the car, when equipped with power steering was entirely —

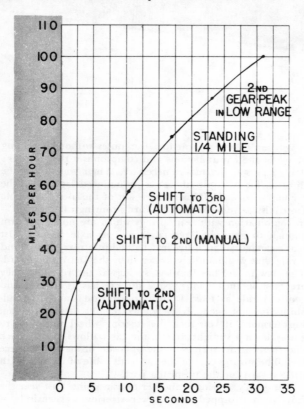

Chart shows results obtained with a gravity accelerometer (Perfometer). Bottom scale is calibrated in miles per hour.

"...a not-quite-sports car that is doing a very real missionary job..."

almost lethally — devoid of feel. This year the feel is pretty acceptable, but the steering is far too slow. In '55 it was none too quick at 3.5 turns from lock to lock. Now it's *really* slow at 4.75 turns. Try to negotiate a complicated maneuver with both hands on the wheel and you get as tied up as if you were in a straightjacket. When the wheel has to spin through hundreds of degrees to aim the car where you want it to go, the only way you can operate is with one hand, and this is steering the hard way. It may not matter much when you're just parking the car or tooling conservatively along mountain roads, but when you become concerned with skids and with vital, sudden changes of direction — as in racing — you need more than the Bird gives you.

Even so, the T-Bird corners remarkably well. When I weighed it I found that with the fuel tank three-quarters full the weight on the front wheels was within five pounds of the weight at the rear. This good balance, plus a low center of gravity and a close tread-to-wheelbase ratio, helps the Bird achieve really excellent road adhesion. For test purposes I use a tight corner that has held some of the fine European sports-touring cars to a ragged 55 mph. But the '56 Bird, in the hands of competition driver Russ Kelly, who ran the test with me, snarled through the turn a good 10 mph faster.

Equally good is the Bird's acceleration. The car has a healthy enough power-to-weight ratio for it to hold its own with many of the world's really fast machines. But you should not attempt full-throttle starts with this car. What you get instead of a quick acceleration time is violent wheelspin.

The power plant with the engine dressup kit. Underhood bright work costs an extra $21.50. This stock Fordomatic engine is rated at 225 hp.

BELOW: Indicating 120 mph on the Bird's clock. Car stayed on high edge of banked course without hands on wheel at this speed. Note light hand control here.

Spare must be tilted back in order to refuel. Tilt mechanism, however, is solid and simple to operate.

A good part of the reason for this behavior is the thrustier horsepower of this year's T-Birds. In '55 all the models had 292 cubic inch engines with 193 advertised horsepower for the stick shift and OD versions and 198 for the car with Fordomatic. Now only the manual shift job has the 292 engine and it's rated at 202 bhp. The Fordomatic and OD cars have engines bored and stroked to 312 cubic inches and are rated at 225 and 215 respectively. My Fordomatic test car did not have the new power kit, which is now available to the public on a very limited basis. It also did not have the competition camshaft and the pair of four-throat carbs that were in Chuck Daigh's car. Without these extras the top speed was not sensational but higher than last year's.

On my own test course, with just a 1.5 mile approach to the timing traps, I was only able to clock an actual 108.7 mph. At the proving ground, under ideal conditions and with a five-mile approach, I got a one-way run of 119.4 mph. Incidentally, at this actual speed the speedometer was

Continued on page 66

This view shows seating position of T-Bird. Adjustable seat and steering wheel allow for various positions of comfort.

T-Bird holds well on standard test curve, but left hairy skid marks. According to author, "It didn't have the glued feel but it stayed stuck and got through the turn faster than some pretty good foreign stuff."

PERFORMANCE
Fordomatic model, 225 bhp

ACCELERATION:

From zero to	Drive range	Low range
30 mph	3.3 secs.	3.2 secs.
40	5.4	4.9
50	8.5	8.0
60	11.7	11.5
70	14.9	14.7
80	20.2	19.8
90	25.2	24.9
100	31.8	31.0
Standing ¼ mile	17.3	17.1
Standing mile	45.4 (average 79.2 mph)	

SHIFT POINTS:
First (automatic)	28 mph (actual)
First (manual)	43 mph (actual)
Second (automatic)	58 mph (actual)

TOP SPEED: (1.5-mile approach to ¼-mile timing trap)
Two-way average	106.4 mph
Fastest one-way run	108.7 mph
With five-mile run	119.4 mph

SPEEDOMETER CORRECTION:
Indicated	Actual
30 mph	27 mph
40	36
50	44
60	53
70	62.5
80	72
90	82
100	91

Three-quarter front view shows new T-Bird to be basically unchanged in body design. Major alterations were accomplished in the steering, engine, and rear springing.

Underchassis shows X braced frame and simple Hotchkiss drive. Front suspension is standard ball joint used on all Fords.

RATING FACTORS:

	Std. trans.	Overdrive	Fordomatic
Bhp per cu. in.	.69	.69	.72
Bhp per sq. in. piston area	2.29	2.37	2.48
Pounds per bhp — test car	——	——	15.8
Piston speed @ 60 mph	1545 fpm	1140 fpm	1430 fpm
Piston speed @ max. bhp	2530 fpm	2640 fpm	2640 fpm
Brake lining area per ton (test car)	——	——	101 sq. ins.

FUEL CONSUMPTION:
Very hard driving	11.3 mpg
Average driving under 60 mph	12.7 mpg

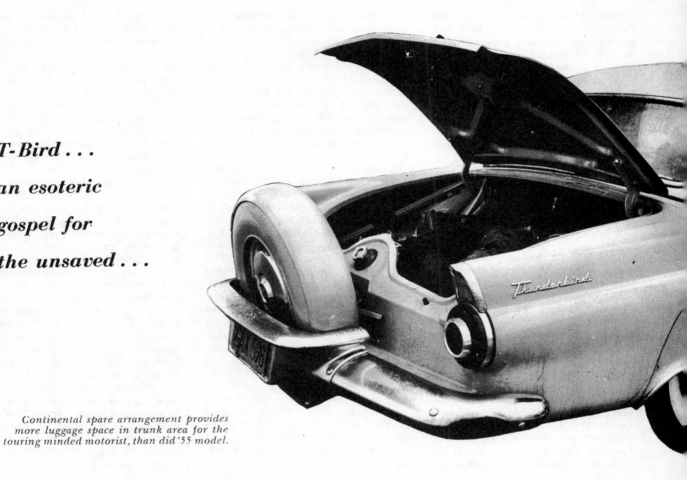

T-Bird . . .

an esoteric

gospel for

the unsaved . . .

Continental spare arrangement provides more luggage space in trunk area for the touring minded motorist, than did '55 model.

SPECIFICATIONS

POWER UNIT:

Type	V8		
Valve arrangement	In-line, pushrod operated		
Idle speed	475 — 500 rpm		
	Std. Trans.	Overdrive	Fordomatic
Maximum bhp	202 @ 4600	215 @ 4600	225 @ 4600
Maximum torque, lb-ft.	289 @ 2600	317 @ 2600	324 @ 2600
Piston displacement	292 cu. in.	312 cu. in.	312 cu. in.
Bore x stroke	3.75 x 3.30 in.	3.80 x 3.44 in.	3.80 x 3.44 in.
Stroke Bore ratio	.88 to 1	.91 to 1	.91 to 1
Compression ratio	8.4 to 1	8.4 to 1	9.0 to 1

DRIVE TRAIN:

Transmission ratios	1st — 2.33	1st — 2.33
	2nd — 1.48	2nd — 1.48
	3rd — 1.00	3rd — 1.00
		OD — 0.70
Final drive ratio	3.73	3.92

CHASSIS:

Suspension, front	Unequal length wishbones, coil springs, ball-joints.
Suspension, rear	Solid axle, torque taken through semi-elliptic springs.
Shock absorbers	Houdaille direct tubular, F & R; 1 in. piston diameter.
Steering type	Worm & two-tooth roller.
Steering wheel turns	4.75 from lock to lock.
Steering turning diameter	36 ft.
Brake type	Hydraulic duo-servo, cast iron drums, 11-in. diam.
Brake lining area	175.5 sq. ins.
Wheel studs	5½-in. studs, 4½" circle diam.
Tire size	6.70 x 15
Rim width (outside)	6.5 ins.
Wheelbase	102 ins.
Tread	56 ins., F & R.

GENERAL:

Length	175 ins.
Width	70 ins.
Height	52.5 ins.
Weight, test car	3550 lbs.
Weight distribution, F/R	50/50

Continued from page **63**

reading 143, the most optimistic error I've come across in a long time and one that the pink-slip jousters would do well to remember. Another good point to remember is that on a car as heavy as the Bird ordinary passenger-car tires are likely to start shedding their threads after 8 or 10 miles of 110 to 115 mph driving. Ford had the cars at the proving ground equipped with Firestone Super Sport tires — tubeless, of course. Under the Bird's hard acceleration the tires slip on the driving wheels and would easily shear the valve stems from conventional tubes. Anyone contemplating serious dragging, using standard tubes would do well to put screws in the wheel rims.

The Bird's brakes are better than they were before. The car I tested last year and this year's test car both had power brakes. In the case of the '55 you could depress the brake pedal a couple of inches and nothing would happen. One sixteenth of an inch more and the wheels would suddenly lock, with assorted embarrassing consequences.

The '56 model's brakes take hold smoothly and evenly. At below 50-mph speeds they lack authority and at 100 mph they seem to serve a sort of token function. These are not the brakes you look for on a sports car or on what the Europeans call a *gran turismo* machine. You learn quickly to downshift to Low Range to add to the car's braking power.

On the whole, the Bird feels quite good at high speed — as good as any loose-steering car can feel. But this and the tendency to dance on its springs makes driving the Bird a more nerve-tightening experience than the average sports car driver is happy to accept.

Another objection that the man who wants a pure sports car is likely to make is that the car has far more iron than it needs. The Bird may be small by Detroit standards but it's unnecessarily bulky and ponderous for a high-performance car. Here again the car's dual personality is the reason. The Bird is based on a shortened version of the Ford convertible frame which, with its rugged cruciform construction, is itself a heavy device. On the Bird this frame is beefed up even more with an immense amount of strap iron that is hand-welded to the bottom of the frame. This iron, two inches wide and half an inch thick, is applied to the side members of the frame and to the four segments of the central X-member. The resulting structure ought to be very rigid and reliable. As a sports car frame it is laughably heavy. As a touring car frame it is ruggedly substantial.

On many other touring-car counts the T-Bird scores very well indeed. It has plenty of room for luggage and passengers. It doesn't have the shoulder-cradling bucket seats that the sports car *aficionado* might prefer, but its yielding upholstery does an above-average job of body bracing. Furthermore, the bench seat is wide enough to accommodate three adults in total comfort or two adults and two kids. The detail work is excellent by any standard, but most important to the American mass market, it meets good U. S. standards of quality, style and comfort. I detected only one jarring note in the luxurious overall effect; cranking the windows up or down is so difficult that you would welcome power assist.

Physically, the '56 Bird, like the '55, is a handsome beast. The biggest styling change this year is, of course, the switch to the continental spare, which makes the car look more like a logical successor to the old Lincoln Continental than the new Continental itself. Naturally the new, external mounting for the spare makes a big difference in the T-Bird's luggage capacity — something all short wheelbase cars can use. In a car that is not essentially a competition machine, the style and utility benefits of this change more than compensate for the small sacrifice in additional wind drag. #

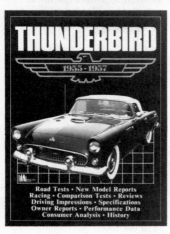
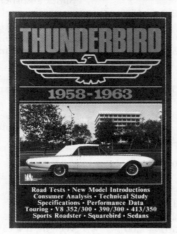
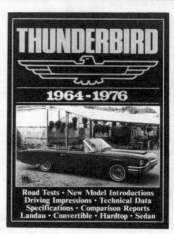

DRIVING
AROUND

with
WALT WORON

'56 THUNDERBIRD AND CORVETTE ROAD TEST

photos by Bob D'Olivo

THE ANNOUNCEMENT BY CHEVROLET that the '56 Corvette would have more power, wind-up windows, and better weatherproofing has, among other things, served to add still more fuel to an old duel. Where the Corvette may not have competed on across-the-board terms with the Thunderbird, the scales are now more evenly balanced. But don't get the idea that Ford has been lulled into a no-progress policy by their sales leadership with the Thunderbird; the No. 1 sales position is hard to come by and is jealously guarded.

To give the best possible comparison between these 2 Detroit-based "sports cars" we thought it best to drive the Thunderbird and Corvette side by side. We wanted the cars to be as alike as possible, but our plans didn't work out quite right: the T-Bird had more initial break-in mileage, which was partially compensated for by its also having power steering and the standard power brakes. It came with the standard plastic top and no soft top, so we (one person can't lift it off without marring the finish) took the top off and then kept both tops down during all testing. **CONTINUED**

Test crew stops at Mt. Wilson to discuss handling of rival cars

Trunk space is somewhat greater in the Thunderbird, at left, but the continental wheel gets in the way. Compartment is much deeper than the Corvette's

Corvette trunk has flat floor with spare tire that is awkward to remove without bumping your head. Despite easy access, there isn't much room

With some prior acclimation to the 2 cars under our belts, 3 of us (Paul Sorber, our new staff member, and Bob D'Olivo, our ace photographer, and I) climbed into the cars before dawn one day and rode off to our desert test site. Alternating between the 2 cars we followed a route that led us thru traffic, over a winding mountain road to the top of 5710-foot Mt. Wilson, then dropped down onto the 2000-foot flatlands of the Mojave Desert. Thru the mountains we were pleased that the heaters worked as well as they did; with tops down we might have otherwise chilled ourselves into going back for the T-Bird's top.

Behind the Wheels the 1st Time

Our 1st reactions to the 2 cars, of course, were those on getting in and out. They are pretty much alike in this respect, with the wraparound support cutting into your kneeroom as you snake in under the wheel. With the top up, it becomes more difficult, for you have to bend down, throw in a leg, duck to miss the top, scoot under the wheel and again avoid the wraparound with your left knee. You should be under-6-foot tall and like setting-up exercises if you'll be driving either car much with the top up.

Once you get in the T-Bird, you'll find the seat is well-padded and comfortable, even for a long trip. On this particular T-Bird the seat rose, lowered, slid forward and backward by electrical power at the touch of a finger control on the door. Within a back-and-forth range of 3 inches, you can adjust the low-set wheel to your liking. Headroom, legroom, and shoulder room are good, but not exceptional.

The Corvette's seat is firmly padded and fits your back contour snugger than the T-Bird because of its semi-bucket shape. Each seat manually adjusts forward and backward, allowing you slightly less legroom than the T-Bird. You're also closer to your passenger, with less shoulder room, but you don't rub against each other. The non-adjustable racing-type, plastic-covered wheel sits close to you and is fairly high.

The T-Bird's instrument panel setup appears to have been thought out with more concern for driver seeability, what with the semi-circular speedometer high on the crash-padded panel, the tach close by and to the left, and the fuel and water temperature gauge below the speedometer.

The Corvette's speedometer, in its above-the-column position, is legible, but the position of the smaller tachometer in the center of the panel makes it almost useless. To see the fuel and water temperature gauges, you have to take your eyes well off the road. The advantage of having oil pressure and ammeter *gauges* instead of warning lights is somewhat lessened by their location on the far side of the centrally located tachometer.

Glove compartments are about a toss-up: the smallish T-Bird's compartment is a far right reach for the driver; the Corvette's upright box, in the center between the seats, is not useful except for the few things you can stack in it.

Chevrolet seems to have come closer to curing windshield distortion, tho some was noticed on the Corvette, the amount in the T-Bird was more annoying. Possibly because of our being closer to the windshield, there seemed to be even more distortion than on Ford sedans. Except for that complaint, and the bubble on the hood of the T-Bird, the cars have equal forward vision. Naturally, with tops down, all-around vision is excellent, marred only by the T-Bird's swivel-type rear view mirror, which can be pushed around to where it doesn't get in the way of forward vision. Glare caused by the blazing sun was noted only occasionally from the T-Bird's spokes. Driving into the sun we praised Ford's foresight in providing narrow, padded visors, and complained about the Corvette's lack of them.

Taking Them Thru Traffic

Our test Thunderbird was more of an in-town car because of its power steering, but if you're of a mind to taint the Corvette's attempt at simon-pure sports car design, you can have it equipped with power steering too. The stiffer steering of the Corvette is one of the features I like about it, tho I dislike winding the wheel 3¾ turns to make a U-turn. Many undoubtedly prefer the driving ease (with a surprising amount of road feel) that the T-Bird's power steering gives it.

Whipping in and out of tight traffic situations, the cars do equally well. Unlike the feeling you get in many small foreign sports cars, you aren't domineered by the big Detroit bullies. The Corvette and Thunderbird are not as small as most sports cars, being little less in width and only a few feet shorter in overall length than their sedan counterparts.

Driving either car in traffic can't be termed an enjoyable experience, for you should have room in front of you to occasionally tromp down hard on the throttle. Not only is this dangerous in town, it'll cause a screech of rubber and possibly more than a raised eyebrow from the local gendarmes. It's more practical to wait until you get to open stretches where it's legally and safely possible to succumb to the urge of getting pushed back in your seat.

How They Go

It took quite a bit of experimenting by all of us to arrive at the best possible shift method for the utmost acceleration. More experimentation, as you would do with a Corvette or T-Bird if it were yours, might possibly trim some time off the figures we got. Those shown in the table indicate the most we could get out of these particular cars using this procedure: revving to 1500 rpm in LOW, holding the car back with the foot brake, then suddenly releasing it and at the same moment stomping the throttle, shifting to DRIVE at 4000 rpm in the T-Bird, and at 5500 rpm in the Corvette. By this method we shaved almost a full second off the 0 to 60 times with the T-Bird using just DRIVE, while we didn't improve the Corvette's time at all. In either car, DRIVE will obviously suffice for normal driving.

From scratch the T-Bird surges ahead, but 2 shifts (from LOW range to intermediate to high) against one (from LOW to DRIVE) for the Corvette allows the latter to catch and barely nose out the T-Bird at the quarter-mile mark. In the passing speed ranges, the Corvette was the Thunderbird's master, even when we tried a manual upshift from LOW to intermediate at 3800-4000 rpm instead of the normal 3400, and higher rpms than the normal upshift at 3800 from intermediate to high. Valves float in the Thunderbird at 4400, not until much over 5600 in the Corvette.

It's a surprising, but undeniably true, fact that neither our test '56 Corvette or Thunderbird had better acceleration across the board than its '55 counterpart. From a standing start neither of them gets off the mark as quick, apparently because of a loading up of the engine by over-carburetion, a characteristic common to most 4-barrel-carbureted engines. When the engines clean out, they make up for some of the time they've lost; thus they get to the quarter-mile quicker, tho they're not going so fast. In high-speed passing the '56 Corvette is faster than the earlier model, but not so the T-Bird. With both '56 cars it could have been a matter of lesser tune, or perhaps the '55s were hotter cars—cars that were made to run like clockwork by each factory's technicians.

The floor-position shift on both Corvette and T-Bird seems quite natural after driving sports cars, which was probably the thinking in placing them there. Both quadrants are well marked; the T-Bird's is lighted at night, tho without driving both cars intermittently as we did, there's not much to confuse you. In the Corvette you can shift from L to D and from D to L with no strain and can't accidentally shift to R because you have to consciously press the lever to the left side and push all the way forward. The T-Bird has an added safety factor in that a knob on top of the lever must be pressed down to allow you to go from D (or N) to R. Unfortunately, this latch permits you to overshift into N when holding the lever in L and manually upshifting to D in trying to get better acceleration times. A modification could be made that would prevent you from going into N without pressing down the button.

An advantage the position of the T-Bird's lever has over the Corvette's is that you can rest your leg against it, at least until it gets too warm. In the Corvette, your throttle foot gets tired because you naturally rest it against the transmission hump, and since the throttle is straight up and down, you're pressing on it with only the ball of your foot. The T-Bird's lever jumped quite a bit on rough roads and vibrated some even on level roads, like the engine mounts were loose. Upshifts and downshifts were quite smooth in both cars.

During these acceleration runs, neither engine detonated and hot starts were easily made. Cold-morning starts were usually quick in the Corvette and took a little cranking in the T-Bird. Neither car heated up, or even got up to 180°F.

Acceleration runs, and mountain driving, always bring out the shortcomings of the brakes, if any. Both systems were quite responsive and could be easily applied with left or right foot. There was some brake fade in the T-Bird, with quick recovery.

Who's Tops in Roadability?

The general feel of the Thunderbird is unlike what you might expect from the car's size and appearance. Thru turns it leans considerably, but after it reaches its maximum point of lean, it settles down and takes the corner quite well. When it breaks loose, which it does after an initial 4-wheel drift, it takes considerable wheel correction and more power to pull out. Despite power steering, it retains a good feel of the road, enough to generally keep you out of trouble.

The Corvette, on the other hand, feels more like a sports car, with more steadiness and not as much apparent lean. The complaint leveled at it in cornering can't be laid to the suspension, which is good and firm, but rather at the carburetors, which starved the engine on a hard left turn; the right bank gets its share, but not the left one. This generally happens about midway in the turn, where you really need it. On right turns it was not quite as bad. The same was noted on the Corvettes at Sebring, except that they starved out in either direction.

When the Corvette's rear end does break loose, it's easier to correct than the T-Bird, tho there are still too many turns from lock to lock for a "sports car." With just one less turn, making it 2¾ lock to lock, you could get thru most turns without changing your grip on the wheel.

To really compare the cornering abilities of both cars, we took them thru the same posted 20-mph right angle (to the right) at 40-45 mph. To compensate for any driver familiarity or error, Sorber and I switched between the 2 cars. For both of us the Corvette stuck in the groove exceedingly well, while the T-Bird drifted across the road, finally breaking loose and several times going off the asphalt.

The Corvette and T-Bird alike have a good sense of direction on perfectly flat, or even crowned, roads. When each leaves the asphalt there is just a slight whipping. Hard frontal and side wind gusts had little effect on either car. Stiffer shocks on the T-Bird would be welcomed by drivers who push their cars more, tho it would stiffen the ride. The wallowing at extremely high speeds (90 and above) makes it somewhat uncomfortable for driving; at lower speeds there's little to concern you. The difference between the 2 cars seems to be in the shocks, for the spring rates of both cars are quite similar.

On choppy asphalt you'll get some wheel vibration in both cars, but you won't hear nor feel any thud in the column. There's no tendency to swap ends on dirt washboard.

How They Compare in Ride

The ride of the T-Bird is definitely softer. The Corvette's ride is more prone to transmit road noises to the driver and

At the same position in the curve, and at identical speeds, the Corvette's better cornering shows up. Thunderbird's greater lean in corners could stand improvement

Dual quad setup dominates Corvette's somewhat roomier under-hood compartment

Thunderbird's engine, hampered with power equipment, is no direct comparison

passenger. The T-Bird has a tendency to "float" over dips and bumps, which is comfortable at low speeds and not as likable at higher speeds.

Both cars bottom on intersection drainage dips if they're driven over at 30 mph or above. After a dip of this type the Corvette recovers its composure quicker. Each had a considerable number of body rattles, while the Corvette also had a vigorous cowl shake on rough roads.

The individual bucket seat of the Corvette is more comfortable for one passenger, but the T-Bird has the advantage of carrying an emergency 2nd passenger in the middle, if he (or she) doesn't mind the transmission hump. The armrest of the Corvette is positioned somewhat better for the passenger, tho with either car it's pleasanter to rest your arm on the doorsill; of course, this isn't the safest practice.

What About Fuel Economy?

Driven over the identical 650 miles, at identical speeds and in identical fashion, the Corvette and T-Bird got virtually identical overall gas mileage. Tho 12.8 and 12.7 may seem unusually low, it's important to remember that we drove the cars hard and fast. Under less strenuous conditions you might expect up to 14-15 mpg, tho if you're like most persons who drive such cars, it will be of little concern—except possibly

for the next time you bench-race. Few competitors are so alike.

And Their Construction?

Fit of the panels on the T-Bird was quite good, except for an occasional ripple in the body. The bumpers are sturdy, more like those of a sedan than those of the Corvette. The workmanship of the Corvette seemed to be on a par with that of the T-Bird. Common to Fiberglas, there were a few cracks in the Corvette's body paint at a few stress points.

Some Final Conclusions

The Thunderbird is pretty much what Ford claims it is—a "personal car," suitable for the bachelor, for the young or "young in heart" couple, or for the husband or wife as a 2nd car. Its sales indicate that the people who are buying it are not necessarily concerned with its sports car attributes, nor are they overly impressed with unbeatable performance. A fact that's sometimes easy to overlook is that pretty big strides have been recently taken by Detroit manufacturers; since the introduction of the T-Bird in the fall of '54, several sedans have surpassed it in acceleration and will stay with it in the handling department. As a "personal car" it meets its requirements. For those who want to make it into a sports car, we would suggest firming it up, adding a good close-ratio gearbox, putting on bigger brakes, and lightening it considerably.

The Corvette is less of a personal car and closer to being, or easily becoming, a sports car. The sales philosophy of Chevrolet seems to have been more to compete with the foreign sports car market—at least until the Thunderbird came along. Now it appears that they're trying to split down the middle by providing more highway comfort for the average guy and/or the ability to make the car into a sports car by the addition of the modification kit (finned brakes, limited-slip differential, disc brakes, and heavy-duty springs).

Which one for you? Within $2.60, you can have your choice. Each performs a slightly different function, and each does right well for itself.

P E R F O R M A N C E

	'56 THUNDERBIRD	'56 CORVETTE
ACCELERATION	From Standing Start 0-60 mph 11.5 seconds ¼-mile 18.0 and 76.5 mph	From Standing Start 0-60 mph 11.6 seconds ¼-mile 17.9 and 77.5 mph
	Passing Speeds 30-50 mph 4.6 seconds 45-60 mph 4.4 50-80 mph 12.8	Passing Speeds 30-50 mph 3.6 seconds 45-60 mph 3.8 50-80 mph 11.0
FUEL CONSUMPTION	Used Mobilgas Special Stop-and-Go Driving 12.7 mpg city and highway average for 650 miles	Used Mobilgas Special Stop-and-Go Driving 12.8 mpg city and highway average for 650 miles

S P E C I F I C A T I O N S

THUNDERBIRD

ENGINE: Piston speed @ max. bhp 2637 ft. per min. Max. bmep 156.6 psi. Additional data in table on page 48.

WEIGHT: Test car weight (with gas, oil, and water) 3600 lbs. Front 1780 lbs. Rear 1820 lbs. Per cent distribution 49.4 front, 50.6 rear. Test car weight/bhp ratio 16.00:1.

PRICES: (Including suggested retail price at main factory, federal tax, and delivery and handling charges, but not freight.) $3147.60.

ACCESSORIES: Fordomatic $215, Overdrive $146, power brakes $34, power steering $64, power windows $70, power seat $65, radio $107, heater $84, convertible top alone $75, with Fiberglas hardtop $290, safety packages $22, $32.

CORVETTE

ENGINE: Piston speed @ max. bhp 2600 ft. per min. Max. bmep 153.6 psi. Additional data in table on page 48.

WEIGHT: Test car weight (with gas, oil, water) 3020 lbs. Front 1610 lbs. Rear 1410 lbs. Per cent distribution 53.3 front, 46.7 rear. Test car weight/bhp ratio 13.42:1.

PRICES: (Including suggested retail price at main factory, federal tax, and delivery and handling charges, but not freight.) $3145.

ACCESSORIES: Prices not yet released for publication.

Even dreamier—even newer

Ford THUNDERBIRD for '56

The newest version of America's most thrilling dream-car-come-true is here...

...ready and waiting to take you places as you've never gone before, in new style that will draw admiring glances wherever you go

One trial spin in the new Thunderbird is enough to quicken the pulse of even the most seasoned driver. You feel you could drive all day ... just enjoying the enormous Thunderbird Y-8 power as it responds to your slightest command! And you can have it with Fordomatic, Overdrive or Conventional Drive.

You can choose power assists to help you steer, stop, control the windows and seat. Cornering never was flatter. The ride was never better. And, depending on your whim, you can have a convertible fabric top or a removable hardtop—or *both*. You feel extra safe, too. For

you know Ford's exclusive Lifeguard Design rides with you.

You feel just a little proud when you pull up at a light. You know that your car's long, low lines are the most distinctive on the road. Interiors sparkle with new color.

And that new rear-mounted spare tire adds as much to the appearance of the car as it does to your luggage space.

These experiences are your everyday fare when you drive a Thunderbird. Why miss them another day?

Flight Testing Ford's Bird

photography: Poole

Road & Track's original slogan was (from 1947 to 1954) "The Motor Enthusiast's Magazine" and this statement is still true today, despite its awkwardness. In accordance with our general policy of dealing primarily with interesting automobiles (which does not necessarily imply that uninteresting cars are impractical) we have allotted considerable space to American cars of the more or less special-interest type.

The mere fact that several special-interest types of cars are even offered by our volume-minded manufacturers is a modern phenomenon, but one which we are happy to find. The Ford Motor Company's Thunderbird is such a car; certainly not in the least bit dull, and appropriately cataloged as a "personal car."

Personal car is the right terminology, for the T-Bird has flown in sports car competition as if its wings were clipped—this is no sports car by any stretch of the imagination, and Ford never claimed otherwise. Furthermore it is now apparent that the Thunderbird's moderate price more than offsets its limited seating capacity, in comparing its sales figures to the luxurious Continental Mark II. While there have been rumors of a T-Bird competition version, the present policy of loading the cars with every conceivable option shows that the motoring enthusiast can go hang, and last year's sales of over 16,000 units proves that Ford found a new market of unsuspected strength.

Evaluating this car in its proper perspective, as a truly luxurious 2-seater convertible, the only conclusion that can be reached is that it succeeds admirably. At the same time our sports car outlook forces us to complain bitterly. It is so similar to a sports car that it seems a shame that it could not at least have been endowed with better steering and handling qualities, both of which are fair to good in comparison to domestic sedans, but abominable for a 2-seater machine.

If performance, without regard to engine displacement, were the only criterion, the Thunderbird would get very high praise. Last year's test (March, 1955) showed very good performance, and the 1956 model, with larger 312 cu. in. engine does even better. Yet

it is true that a well known imported sports car with 100 less cu. in. will readily out-perform the best that Dearborn engineers can produce. In this respect our test car had, as last year, the automatic transmission. Despite all our efforts, we were unable to find a stick-shift Thunderbird within a 500 mile radius of our test strip.

As last year, we employed our "forced-shift" technique and this cuts the 0-60 mph and standing ¼ mile times by about .5 second. Normally the Ford automatic upshifts at a mere 3600 rpm but all the data recorded was made using 4500 rpm as a limit in 1st and 2nd gears. This is accomplished by starting in "LO" range, shifting to "DRIVE" at an idicated 43 mph, back to LO at 50 mph, and finally to DRIVE again at 80 mph.

On starting from a standstill, there is a definite pause before the car moves off. This is caused by slippage in the torque convertor (and not by rear spring windup) and does not affect the times recorded as our procedure does not start the watches until the first foot of car movement. Trick starts, such as holding the brake on, or racing the engine in neutral before pulling the lever into LO, give spectacular wheel-spin but no time improvement. When the throttle is depressed the Thunderbird rear end drops and the car moves off like a hydroplane getting up on its step. An honest 60 mph required an indicated 68 and our data showed an average of 9.3 seconds required, from 0-68, with one trial at 9.0 seconds dead.

The highest speedometer reading seen was 120 mph, during the best one-way timed run of 113.9 actual mph. The tachometer read 4600 rpm at the time and would go no higher, even with 5 miles available for peaking-out. Obviously this car was well tuned (by Bill Stroppe, well known Ford specialist) and the odometer showed 2300 miles at the time of the test. At this speed, the car was easy to control and high speed stability is excellent.

The twisting road characteristics of the Thunderbird might be described as Allard or Dellow-like, but with a difference. At the curb, with full tank, there is 60 lbs more weight on the rear wheels than in front. Two adults put the rear end weight up to 52.5% of the total. Accordingly the tail tends to swing out on

The Thunderbird Y-8 is smooth, quiet, dependable, powerful and crowded with accessories.

The spare tire must be tilted back and the trunk lid opened, before fuel can be added.

corners and the combination of very slow (4.3 turns) steering with a power booster and much too soft rear springs makes safe control questionable. However there is ample warning of too vigorous cornering by virtue of the rear tires rubbing on something when the body begins to roll. The power-steering is unobtrusive in normal driving, but lacks feel when cornering. We also found that a tricky corner entered conservatively could produce exciting results when the throttle was depressed to accelerate out. There is tremendous power available and any such car must always be treated with respect, especially by the throttle foot. In this case the tendency of the transmission to downshift could easily produce a spin-out and in general it appears to be wiser to confine cornering experiments to LO range (second gear, above 20 mph.)

The Thunderbird has 11″ brake drums with 170 sq. in. of lining area, enough for any car driven in average fashion and weighing under 4000 lbs., loaded. However the combination of a vacuum booster, which makes for a deceptively light pedal pressure, and an over 100 mph performance is not too fortunate. One moderate stop from over 100 mph produced signs of fade and two such stops within 3 minutes gave genuine fade and pungent odors. At this point there were still brakes, but pedal pressure was perhaps doubled. Despite all this we feel that no one would be foolish enough to drive this car for long at 100 mph, if only because of its original equipment tires.

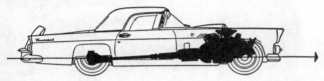

The Thunderbird engine is placed well behind the front wheels.

The bench type seat is wide enough for three adults except that the large transmission tunnel allows no room for the middle passenger's legs. Although the seats are very close to the floor, driving the car is comfortable due to the fact that either foot can be used for braking. The adjustable steering is a real boon but anyone over 5′-10″ finds that the legs tend to hit the wheel when it is pushed well forward in Italian G.P. style.

As is usual with American cars, we quote the lowest basic list price. In this case the $3163.10 is for a bare car with stick-shift and hard top, although our test car had the following extras:

Fordomatic	$215.00
Soft top	290.30
Radio & heater	190.60
Power steering	64.00
Power seats	64.50

This adds up to $3987.50, to which freight and local taxes must be added.

The Thunderbird is a well-made, high performance automobile and fully justifies its title of "Personal Car." ●

The hard top is easily removed by two people and the new spare tire mounting gives a worthwhile increase in trunk volume.

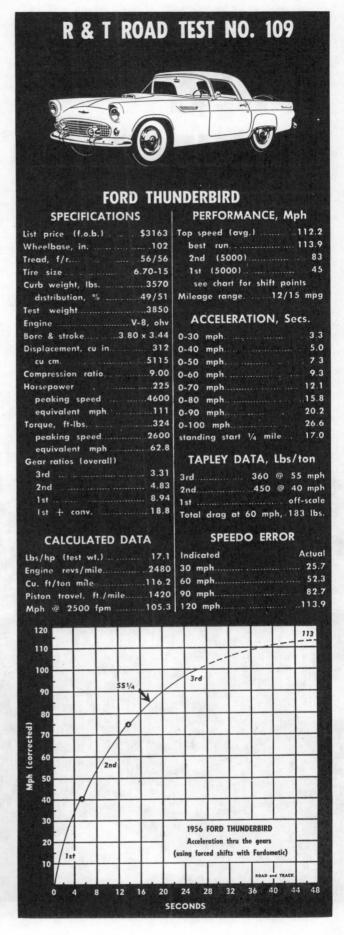

R & T ROAD TEST NO. 109

FORD THUNDERBIRD

SPECIFICATIONS

List price (f.o.b.)	$3163
Wheelbase, in.	102
Tread, f/r	56/56
Tire size	6.70-15
Curb weight, lbs.	3570
distribution, %	49/51
Test weight	3850
Engine	V-8, ohv
Bore & stroke	3.80 x 3.44
Displacement, cu in.	312
cu cm.	5115
Compression ratio	9.00
Horsepower	225
peaking speed	4600
equivalent mph	111
Torque, ft-lbs.	324
peaking speed	2600
equivalent mph	62.8
Gear ratios (overall)	
3rd	3.31
2nd	4.83
1st	8.94
1st + conv.	18.8

PERFORMANCE, Mph

Top speed (avg.)	112.2
best run	113.9
2nd (5000)	83
1st (5000)	45
see chart for shift points	
Mileage range	12/15 mpg

ACCELERATION, Secs.

0-30 mph	3.3
0-40 mph	5.0
0-50 mph	7.3
0-60 mph	9.3
0-70 mph	12.1
0-80 mph	15.8
0-90 mph	20.2
0-100 mph	26.6
standing start ¼ mile	17.0

TAPLEY DATA, Lbs/ton

3rd	360 @ 55 mph
2nd	450 @ 40 mph
1st	off-scale
Total drag at 60 mph	183 lbs.

CALCULATED DATA

Lbs/hp (test wt.)	17.1
Engine revs/mile	2480
Cu. ft/ton mile	116.2
Piston travel, ft./mile	1420
Mph @ 2500 fpm	105.3

SPEEDO ERROR

Indicated	Actual
30 mph	25.7
60 mph	52.3
90 mph	82.7
120 mph	113.9

1956 FORD THUNDERBIRD
Acceleration thru the gears
(using forced shifts with Fordomatic)

ROAD and TRACK

A NEW THUNDERADO

... the shape of things to come

In styling, workmanship, unusual details, and advanced features, this genuine Florida custom is full of future promises

Photos by Frank Boran

IT OFTEN is claimed that customized or restyled cars anticipate or precede designs in production. There is abundant evidence to support such a contention and no better case can be made than the beautiful vehicle shown on these pages and on the cover of this issue of MOTOR LIFE. It can be truly said that here is one of the shapes of things to come.

The work is that of Clark Alexander, of Miami, Florida, who says approximately 18 months and some $15,000 went into the job. The styling can best be summed up as the kind that might be expected if Cadillac elected to develop something in the Thunderbird field, or if the T-Bird were to borrow features from the Eldorado. Most apparent, of course, are the headlights, fins, windshield and interior as being derived from these two cars. Yet the Thunderado should rightly be classed as an original custom, since a large percentage of its metal work is from fresh stock.

In addition to the advanced styling touches, however, the Thunderado is an example of the smaller (by U.S. standards) and more compact automobile which ultimately will be taken up by Detroit. Its wheelbase, for instance, is 10 inches shorter than the present standard in the low-priced field. Some of its other details amount to genuine innovations, as a study of the closeups will prove. All these, plus superb workmanship, makes Alexander's Thunderado one of the finest. •

Thunderbird units include windshield, dash, steering and seats. Floor gear lever is hooked to Hydra-Matic. Body is designed to accept T-Bird's soft or hard top.

The body formed by hand is only three feet high at the cowl. Chassis is standard Ford, shortened to wheelbase of 104 inches.

When viewed from any angle, the Thunderado is beautifully styled, neatly compact. Rear deck lid of car is one solid piece and access to luggage space (see next page) is from behind the seat backs. Both the front and rear bumpers are carefully modified Cadillac. Before turning to the next page, take a good look at the recessed glass license plate holder.

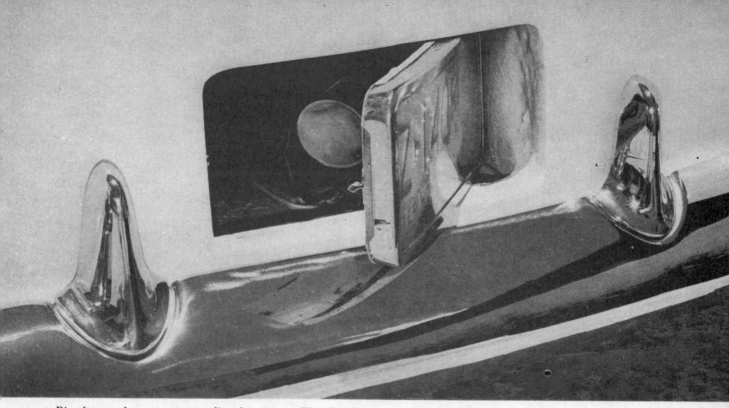

Big closeup shows two outstanding features on Thunderado. First, note clever and unusual method of concealing the gas intake behind a swiveling license frame. Next, workmanship is pointed up by smooth job of insetting guards into bumper.

Power source has not been overlooked, is a sturdy and potent '55 Cad V-8. Although it sets in Ford frame, transmission and rear end also are standard Hydra-Matic and Cadillac units.

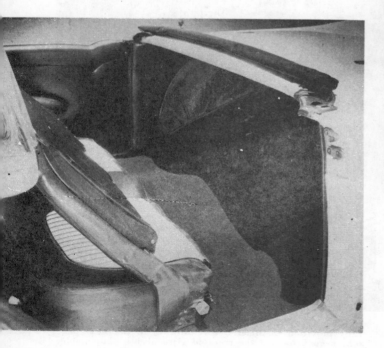

Since deck lid is solid, luggage compartment entry is by tilting forward the seat back. This is becoming more common, may forecast solution when Detroit goes to retracting tops.

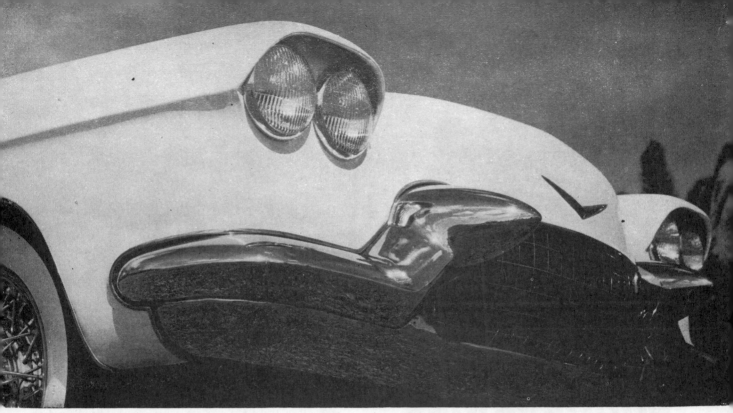

Dual headlights are General Electric's 5½-inch size—with one lens tilted slightly lower than the other to provide both distance and road illumination. Neat mating of the bumper units and trimmed edges of body metal indicate extreme care.

Hood and fenders are one piece and break forward from rest of the body along the decorative horizontal strip, the only side trim on the front section. Lifting of the hood is by hydraulic power (another coming feature). A most unusual touch, of course, is the way the nose is contoured around the stationary grille and bumper. Grille is reworked '55 Cadillac.

Pair of 1957 Thunderbirds show off major changes from last year. Grille has been slightly enlarged, the bumpers are heavier, fins have been added and the rear deck stretched out.

The spare tire, carried on a continental mount for '56, has been returned to the interior of the enlarged trunk, where it started out in 1955. In general, the car looks better than ever.

THE 1957
THUNDERBIRD

STYLING—Moderate facelift, with revamped grille and bumpers, bigger trunk. The spare tire has gone back inside again.

PERFORMANCE—Not much improvement found in prototypes, but later production models should be up considerably.

ENGINEERING—Just a few changes in frame, brakes, springs. Overall length less. And 14-inch wheels and tires adopted.

BODY TYPES—Same as before, one body with choice of soft top or removable hardtop. Rumored four-seater some time away.

THE tremendous public acceptance of the Thunderbird was the big reason for Ford exploiting it via the "kissin' cousin" route to help sell standard Ford passenger cars. This automobile, universally and affectionately known as the "T-Bird," has achieved popularity that can't be measured by normal sales standards. Why? And will it continue to rate as highly in 1957? Let's see:

BY KEN FERMOYLE

LIKE NEARLY everyone else in the country I've been smitten by the Thunderbird since it first appeared. Earlier, really, since I was introduced to it before most people. It goes without saying then, that I was very anxious to see what had been done to it for 1957.

I was rather pleased after I first saw it early in the summer that it was still to be definitely a T-Bird—if you know what I mean. Frankly, however, I'm still partial to the original 1955 jobs. That's the trouble with success; it's *so* hard to top!

As far as styling changes for '57 are concerned, you'll have to judge for yourself whether the results are good or bad. There have been quite a few but they don't make a major difference in the total effect of the car. Most of them, naturally, have been aimed at keeping the T-Bird within kissin' kinship of the Ford passenger car line. (You might not agree with that, but it's important to Ford.)

The front bumper and grille have been revamped. Front wheel cutouts have been changed—and some bright-metal trim added to the formerly chrome-less side as a result. The body has been extended some 5 inches at the rear, but the spare tire has been moved back inside the trunk where it belongs! (In fact, the reason for the lengthened deck was to permit just that. Dearborn heard plenty about the continental mount!)

The contour of the deck lid has been reworked; it's higher now and has a reverse angle at the rear. Rear quarter panels have been restyled along '57 Ford passenger car lines. They feature the "canted blade" or fin effect along with the huge tail lights of the standard Fords.

There have been fewer changes in the chassis to which this sheet metal is bolted. Fewer, really, than in Ford passenger cars. The frame is unchanged except that number four cross member is now a box rather than channel section (because of the longer deck and extra weight).

Front suspension is virtually the same as in earlier models. Ball joints and coil springs are still used.

Semi-elliptic springs are retained at rear, but five leaves are now used. (There were four last year.) They are the same length (55 inches) and width (2 inches).

Effective brake lining area has been increased from a fraction under 170 inches to 176 inches, despite the switch to 14-inch tires and wheels. This was done by enlarging front brake area slightly, keeping rear brakes the same size as last year.

Wheelbase is the same—102 inches—and tread is still 56 inches front and rear. Overall length has gone from 185.12 inches to 182.01—but this is deceiving. As mentioned earlier

With the spare back in the trunk, the T-Bird still has more luggage space than in the past. This is possible because of increased length. The Bird now looks less like a sports car.

Engine modifications have been few, although output is now up to a top rating of 245 (which is optional with stick shifts). New four-barrel arb here with air cleaner off is lower.

the body is some 5 inches longer; last year's overall figure included the tacked-on continental tire mounting. Overall height is down from 52.14 to 51.54 inches with the hardtop in place (from 52.50 to 51.90 with soft top), due principally to the smaller tires.

In engines, the 312-cubic-inch V-8, standard on Ford-O-Matic and overdrive models, is rated at 245 hp with 9.7-to-1 compression ratio. This engine is 265 hp when equipped with optional four-barrel carburetor. A 292-cubic-inch V-8 is standard on standard shift models, is rated at 212 hp with 8.6-to-1 compression. However, the bigger engine is optional on the manual shift T-Birds.

So much for the tangibles. What's more important to T-Bird admirers is how these changes have affected the car on the road. That's what I was anxious to find out when I slipped behind the wheel of an engineering prototype out at Ford's Dearborn proving grounds.

The job I drove was one used to check out the engineering changes for 1957. It was standard '57 all the way thru except for a few unimportant pieces of chrome. Unfortunately, it was a fully-equipped model—power seats, windows, brakes, steering, Ford-O-Matic; the works—and had covered a lot of long, hard miles. Perhaps that's why the performance wasn't up to my expectations.

But let's take handling first:

The T-Bird is no sports car and Ford has never made that claim. It has, however, been a car which put a lot of the fun back into driving. It still is.

If anything, the changes made for '57 have improved handling. Weight distribution is better due to the extra poundage added at the rear by the longer body. Engineer Jim Aldridge of the Thunderbird development group, who rode with me, said their tests indicated that rear end stability was improved as a result. I'm inclined to agree.

There seemed to be less rear end steering effect in hard cornering; the difference wasn't great, but it was there. Of course, a few short hours driving isn't conclusive proof but I can certainly say that the '57 T-Bird handles at least as well as its predecessors and be accurate.

My major handling complaint is—again—the very slow steering. It requires nearly 4½ turns of the wheel to go from lock to lock—even with power steering. It would seem that if they must use this power assist, they could at least lower the steering ratio in cars so equipped. As it is, you're kept pretty busy getting thru a tight radius turn.

In general, the Thunderbird still falls somewhere between a true sports car and a standard passenger car as far as overall handling and maneuverability are concerned.

The same is pretty much true about the ride. It certainly can't be called harsh or uncomfortable. Going from a normal sedan to a T-Bird, you might notice a little extra firmness and a shade more pitch due to the shorter wheelbase—not, however, if your sedan was more than four or five years old.

You get an extra measure of comfort in the new T-Birds as a result of a new seat design, by the way. It doesn't look much different than seats in earlier models, but the development engineers swear by it. They claim it is a big help in reducing fatigue on long trips in particular.

Now we get to performance; and, frankly, it was disappointing. The car tested just didn't deliver the acceleration you expect from a T-Bird. (Probably, however, the production models will be much better.) Top speed would almost certainly have been better; unfortunately there are no facilities for maximum speed runs at Ford's Dearborn test area.

Let me give you the figures I got first, then we'll look at some of the *whys* behind them. (Figures quoted were the result of stopwatch timing with the speedometer corrected for error. All runs were on a dead-level straight.)

Best I could do from 0 to 60 mph was 11.5 seconds. From 0 to 70 took 16 seconds. (This time was for a one-way run only; all others are two-way averages.) From 0 to 80 took 21.2 seconds and the 50 to 80 time was 15.1 seconds. Only low and intermediate were used from 0 to 60 and 70 mph but I had to shift into high range just over 70 which accounted for the long time it took to get up to the 80 mph notch. The 50 to 80 runs were made by running in drive range and just flooring the throttle to get into intermediate. Downshifting to low—and thus going into intermediate and being able to hold it there longer—might have cut the time but I wanted to simulate normal highway conditions.

One of the big reasons for the relatively lackluster low- and mid-range performance was the axle ratio. It has been lowered (a higher gear) from 3.31 in '56 to 3.10 with Ford-O-Matic. With three-speed manual transmission the change is from 3.73 to 3.56; with overdrive, from 3.92 to 3.70. And, as the specification table shows, there isn't a lot more horsepower than last year. (There is also some added weight.)

Top speed will undoubtedly be better especially compared to '56 models which had the added drag of the outside tire mounting. Economy will probably be slightly better too. ●

SCI

Thunderbird for '57 has been redesigned and reengineered with more power than ever before . . . it's also further from Sebring than ever before.

DRIVERS REPORT: the 1957 Thunderbird

Basic T-Bird body lines are still visible. Heavier bumper-grille and flared fender add flash.

By KARL LUDVIGSEN

YOU don't have to be told first—a quick glance at a Thunderbird instantly reveals its ancestry. The first Bird prototype was based on a shortened standard Ford chassis for exploratory purposes. This was a valid start, and later versions never wandered very far from this concept. For production and servicing ease, it made sense to build a Bird out of the FoMoCo parts bins. Sense or not, this goes a long way toward explaining the nature of Ford's "personal car."

As indicated in Sports Cars Illustrated's road test of the 1956 Thunderbird, the car is a compromise resulting from sports car looks on a workday chassis. Ford's interpretation of the appeal of the sports car puts emphasis on the exclusive feel of two small seats in a big automobile. They enhanced this in 1956 by hanging the spare tire out back, and for 1957 the major change has been the grafting on of long canted tail plumage for the Bird. The spare has been tucked back inside, and with it have gone a lot of

trunk access problems.

The additional rear overhang was handsomely handled, and the bumper treatment is pleasantly clean. It all contains a huge luggage compartment which is marred only by the inward-angled spare tire. The fuel filler has been moved from the center to the right side to exploit the new space further.

A clever tie-in was achieved by curling the fender peaks around the door-handles, while the new front bumper-grille has a commercially massive look. Otherwise the sheet-metal is unchanged, but with the louvered wheel discs this is probably the jauntiest T-Bird yet. And we haven't even mentioned the greatly expanded color range, which includes two exclusive Bird colors: light pink and metallic copper.

If the hardtop portholes have started to pall, an unpunctured version is optional equipment. Clamping for the hardtop has been revised, and the convertible mechanism modified to make operation considerably easier. Two years'

Latest squat Holley 4-barrel is wide open & spread out. Choke on primary is visible, as are separated float chambers. Throttle linkage heavy & complex for shift control.

Bird interior is handsome and safe, but tach is low at left. Dished wheel and dash pad are standard.

exact position pre-selected on the two dials. The T-Bird is not hard to get in and out of, but this gimmick ensures that the entry condition will always be the best possible. Moreover, if husband and wife both use the car they can avoid groping for the proper location by pre-setting their personal combination. If this were a sports car we would laugh, but it's a neat tailoring trick for a personal car. It's also a harbinger of similar gadgets for lower standard cars.

Power assists are again optional for the side windows, but the padded panel and sun visors are now standard. Covering materials have been chosen to give maximum windshield glare, and instrument lights are completely shielded by a wide, deep cowl. The dials themselves are handsomely round and fully visible with the wheel in straight-ahead position. In a turn, the horn ring suddenly confuses things. The sweep-second clock and the 5000 rpm

experience has also led to heavier door hinges. Seats in the old Thunderbird never won much praise, and without any change in shape or bulk the new ones have been made much more comfortable. Separate sections for driver and passenger are sprung to give much better adaptation to the spine and deceptively good side support. Cushioning over the drive shaft has been retained to make life easier for a third passenger.

Interior adjustability has always been a good Bird feature, and the engineering prototype we drove at the Detroit proving grounds had the adjustable steering wheel and four-way power seats. It didn't have the new Dial-O-Matic seat control which is, nevertheless, worth mentioning. This is controlled from the dash by two concentric numbered knobs: one for horizontal and one for vertical positioning.

When the ignition is turned off the seat automatically moves as far back and down as it can go. Turning on the ignition causes the seat to move forward and up to the

Those tail-lights will be blinding but visible, and the concentric backup light is neat. Exhaust is well integrated.

T-Bird —

tachometer are welcome, but the latter is hidden away on the lower left and could easily be relocated upwards.

Another clever trick for an open car is incorporated in the radio control. Its volume is sensitive to car speed—allowing a louder setting for wind noise which diminishes in the quiet of city traffic. (No annoying blasting at traffic lights.) The right-hand side of the dash is basically unchanged, retaining its good-sized glove compartment.

The driving position is generally good, and the big dished steering wheel is nicely angled. There's just enough leg room and plenty of width, but with both standard and power brakes there's a big level difference between accelerator and brake which can cause some discomfort. Although the rear view mirror forms a forward blind spot, vision all around is adequate.

Thunderbird development engineers are primarily interested in improving the ride of their "light" car, and to this end they were glad to move the pendulum weight of the spare tire back inboard. This has reduced pitching, and small bumps are well damped out. With the improvement in seating, the Bird's space and comfort factors rate very high.

Organization-wise the Thunderbird is now an independent Ford product and the car's structure now differs greatly from the wide, sketchy frame adopted for the low 1957 line. The heavily bolstered crossmember chassis is retained as is the coil front suspension. After a digression to four leaves in 1956, the rear springs are back to five leaves again. Shocks are basically the same but incorporate new valving.

A big change, and one which we were curious about, is the adoption of 14 inch tires and safety-rim wheels. Unfortunately, these were carrying only standard pressure as we wheeled the Bird over the serpentine Ford handling course. The factory engineer was remarking on the superior handling of the '57 car—we could just hear him above the anguished howling from the tires.

To be fair, the T-Bird didn't stick too badly, and the previously skittish rear end didn't act up at all. Understeer was there in big quantities; the wheel having to be wound well over to hold the car on line. Front/rear stability is somewhat better than be-

fore, but at the recommended pressures the overall traction is not outstanding and the car is somewhat of a handful. Power steering was welcome for all that twirling, and the Ford system is a good compromise between road feel and minimum effort. There are still well over four turns to be made, though, and once the car is lost the only way out is an ejection seat.

We didn't pound the brakes too hard, but did notice that the power boost would be a worthwhile accessory. Pedal pressure was definitely high for the resulting stopping power. Brake drum diameters for '57 remained at 11 inches, but a lining area increase is claimed as a result of widening the front secondary shoes. This seems to have stabilized the action of the self-energizing mechanism; a valuable step in reducing fade.

Basic engine options start with a 292 cubic inch V-8 for the standard shift version. This carries a 9.1 to one compression ratio and babbit mains and with a two-barrel carburetor delivers 212 hp at 4500 rpm. If overdrive or Fordomatic is ordered, 312 cubic inches are supplied. This puts out 245 horses at 4500 rpm on a 9.7 to one compression ratio, and copper-lead bearings are used. Holley produced a new low silhouette four-barrel carb for these cars which is exceedingly open and compact and challenges the fuel-injection boys for lowness. Its housing is the very thin replaceable-paper-element air filter; one wingnut takes this all apart.

New transom treatment has expanded Bird trunk, but spare intrudes.

Our engineering hack had the standard Fordomatic combination, with the now-familiar floor control quadrant. Properly used, of course, this can hold the gearbox in each of its three forward speeds as long as desired. To review briefly, low is held by leaving the lever in "L" position. The shift to second is made by moving the lever to 'D", and that gear can be held by returning again to "L". Finally, high is reached by going up to "D" again. Our Fordomatic linkage was set to

upshift at roughly 4000 rpm which corresponded to 30 mph in low and 57 in second.

Sports Cars Illustrated's test procedure is to click the watch as the throttle is punched, which accurately reproduces real operating conditions. This properly penalizes the sloppy automatics, and in this case, the time from zero to 30 was a mediocre 4.9 seconds. Using more extreme methods, our 1956 test produced a figure of 3.3 seconds which the newer car, being all of five pounds lighter, should be able to duplicate.

Allowing the box to shift for itself we moved on up to 50 in 9.3 seconds and to 60 in 12.7. With real clutches the Ford test drivers are running much closer to 10 seconds to 60, and deducting 1.6 seconds for the Fordomatic's bashfulness our time reduces to 11.1 seconds. This is a logical improvement over last year's 11.5 figure.

With preview and test traffic glutting the proving grounds, higher speeds weren't possible, but the engineers estimate a reasonable 116 miles per hour top speed for the Bird. Throughout it all, the V-8 spun with a competent whir and dug in nicely when it picked up revs. A modified manifold and bigger intake valves contribute to this, as does a new camshaft, but idling remains dead smooth at 600 rpm. The exhaust note is clean and not too blatty.

At the last minute Ford has announced two "Corvette Chaser" engine options. The "special high performance" and the "special extra-high performance" put out 270 and 285 hp, respectively. Compression ratios are 9.7 to one and two four-barrels are clamped on. No fuel injection is hinted at, but it's significant that Holley has acquired all U. S. rights to the long-developed English Lucas system. This has powered the factory D-type Jaguars to some impressive performances lately, and is simple enough to be suitable for Detroit. The engineers admit that they've been working on it, but fuel economy is still a problem.

Final refinements for 1957 include gas tank capacity up three gallons from last year's seventeen, and a completely new rear axle with straddle-mounted pinion. Ford has kept an open ear to customer wants in this very specialized line and its product should now be well in tune with demand. Sales so far seem to be a function of production, anyway, the target for this year being 20,000 units and over. As a comfortable, rakish, exclusive road machine, the T-Bird is a nice package, and it's farther from Sebring than ever.

—*Karl Ludvigsen*

Impressions of the T-Bird

FORD'S PRODIGY IS A GENTLEMAN'S HIGH-PERFORMANCE COUPÉ

TO the list of rare birds seldom seen in this country and whose habits are largely unknown might be added Ford's inappropriately named Thunderbird. This silent, sleek and colourful product is often wrongly classified over here; because it is low, powerful and has no rear seats it is assumed to be a sports car, which was not, I think, the maker's intention.

First, a word or two about its features. The T-Bird was introduced in October, 1954; the model under discussion here closely resembles the latest version in America. The engine is a 225 b.h.p. V-8 unit, and it has Ford's own automatic transmission. Ignoring for a moment the external mounting of the spare wheel, the lines are as clean and pleasing as any that have left America since the war. There is the minimum of non-functional ornamentation, and the bumpers are single slabs. The coupé body style, with much-wrapped-round screen, caters for all climatic conditions because the hard top of plastic construction is quickly detachable for good weather and a hood, totally enclosed when folded, is also fitted for shower protection.

When the hard top is fitted the car is no different from a fixed-head coupé. It is sound- and weather-proofed, quiet and roomy. Heating and ventilation are adequately catered for. The inharmonious optional portholes are very valuable in removing a considerable blind spot when reversing and parking.

Returning to the spare wheel, reminiscent of classy Continental sports coupés of the 1930s, this was provided more to meet popular demand than because the makers thought it was right. It is claimed to give the car a traditional touch and incidentally takes a little weight to the back, where it is welcome. In America the demand for this kind of wheel mounting is such that more than one accessory manufacturer supplies parts for converting various models to carry one or a brace of wheels in tins at the back. The overhang in some cases is remarkable.

For reasons unknown, I first approached the T-Bird on the defensive: I wanted it to be a Hollywood nonsense instead

of an enterprising and soundly engineered model from Detroit; perhaps the salmon pink colour was off-putting. By the end of its visit to my "stable" I was very sorry indeed to see it go. Of course, it is a luxury to have a car of this size and power to carry two or three people. This was a special equipment model, and I freely confess to being childishly delighted with the various electrical devices. If a pair of neat two-way, two-plane switches can be made to cause the seat to move smoothly forward or backward and up or down on a production car, I would prefer not to press a catch and shuffle myself about in an undignified manner. On wide cars, where passenger-side window winders are out of reach, there is much to be said for electrical operation of these as well. Many a risky swerve follows an attempt to drive and wind a window at the same time.

But all the gimmicks in the world would not make a bad

A pleasant traffic car and not too un-handy even in London's narrow streets and congestion

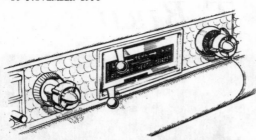

Left: Heater and de-froster controls

Right: Electric-seat adjustment control. Below is the padded safety roll which runs round the cockpit sides and front

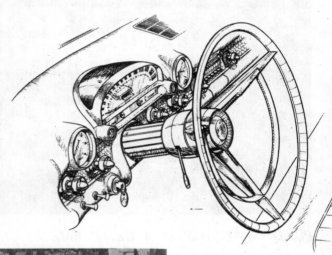

car desirable, so let us consider the basic vehicle again. The automatic transmission selector lever is placed on the floor like a sports car gear shift. The decision to put it there must confound all the arguments *re* column change, push buttons and the rest. It has the usual position for Park, Reverse, Neutral, Drive and Lo. The box with which it is associated makes a large mound in the middle of the floor, but width and floor space are such that three grown-ups can still sit comfortably. On one occasion I squeezed in two grown-ups, each with a child in front of them, as well as me at the wheel.

When one engages drive and puts the accelerator foot down the engine winds up healthily and the r.p.m. indicator reaches around 1,800 at once. This is getting towards maximum torque for the V-8. The car surges forward, catching up with the r.p.m. with the help of the hydraulic torque converter. Then, according to the amount of throttle, the gear changes almost imperceptibly into the higher ratios at between 20 and 65 m.p.h. The lower the power and slower the speed on changing, the less can be heard or felt of the change.

To change down (below the maximum speed for Lo) you kick-down on the accelerator and the change is smooth and almost instantaneous. I do not remember a silkier or more pleasing automatic box than the Fordomatic on the Thunderbird. With so much power available, losses here and there are unimportant and the car has a very rapid acceleration at all speeds up to about 90 m.p.h., and even there it continues quickly enough up to well over 100 m.p.h. I did not exceed "the ton" myself.

Under nearly all conditions the car handles very sweetly

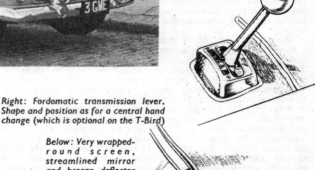

Above: A smart grouping of dials in front of the driver. Note the transparent hood over the day-lit speedometer, and adjustable, dished wheel

Left: Low and long, the T-Bird looks small from outside but, from the driving seat, there appears to be a great deal of car in front

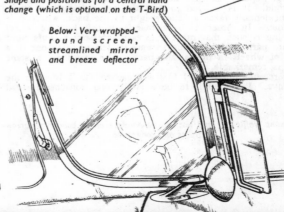

indeed. The steering is very light and pleasing, though for British use it could be higher geared with advantage and still be light enough. The lock is adequate. Cornering is a lot better than you think it is going to be. There is little roll, no great tyre squeal, and with a touch of power on the way round a fast turn can be held comfortably. I did not try handling the car—a precious and hard-worked demonstrator—to its limits in greasy weather, but in normal London wet it caused no concern at all. The straight and level ride is soft but firm; that is to say, there is no float, but neither does one feel road vibrations and bumps. Only at very high speeds does it start to come to the limits of its patience, and even then the driver would usually have had enough before the car showed any vices. Low-geared steering is a handicap on any car when trying to correct skids or check an emergency swerve.

Braking is very good in the American sense. The servo-aided pedal load is very light, the brakes pull you up evenly and without squeal and, for a crash-stop in traffic, as when a child or dog dashes out between vehicles, the effect is terrific. The

Right: Fordomatic transmission lever. Shape and position as for a central hand change (which is optional on the T-Bird)

Below: Very wrapped-round screen, streamlined mirror and breeze deflector

Impressions of the T-BIRD . . .

soft linings that help to make this possible, together with shrouded, little-cooled drums, result in a marked reduction in efficiency if one "drives on the brakes" for a fast mile or two as European owners often will. I have no doubt that cooling air could easily be scooped or ducted in and hard linings fitted (complete with cold squeal) for a hard-driving owner.

Reverting to static characteristics, one would have expected a huge boot on a relatively large coupé, but this is not one of the Thunderbird's lavish features. The styling would not suffer —it might well be improved—by another 6in of boot (less exterior spare) and a later curve down at the rear end. By American standards the car is quite short.

Safety styling inside this and others of their cars earned the Ford company a prize not long ago. It includes a dished steering wheel, safety door catches and padded ribs around facia and doors. The steering column is adjustable for length but the range, even with seat full back, provides only "near" or "very near"—and I am no more than averaged sized. If I were looking for another point to criticize I should mention the control knobs which, while substantial and sensibly shaped themselves, seem flimsily mounted or attached.

The grouping of instruments ahead of the driver is pleasing and well carried out. The hood over the speedometer is neat, as is the arrangement for daylight illumination from behind. I particularly coveted the radio, which seemed so much better than others I have tried. Tone and volume control were excellent; it had manual or push-button control and in addition self-tuning both for town and country. The speakers were beautifully clear and true and, of particular importance to a city driver, interference was practically nil. Trolley-buses passed without a hiss or crackle, bridges hardly produced fade at all, close, high buildings might not have been there and—my *bête rouge* in the form of a particular tailor's neon sign in South London, could produce no riveting noises at all while I waited, as usual, for a change of traffic signal.

Among the other comforts of the T-Bird which I recall are the adjustable speed suction wipers which are excellent, except when following lorries on muddy roads. These particular blades did not quite stop when the car was accelerating to overtake through grimy spray, but they came very close to it. In the rain the wrapped-round extremities of the screen keep reasonably clear, but if one sits well into the outside corner of the seat and thus looks along rather than through them, there is quite a lot of distortion, wet or dry.

However, we all make some sacrifices for appearance. I make some for patriotic reasons, too, and I do not expect to own that wide expanse of piped red leather which is the Thunderbird's inviting seat, or the fascinating vehicle around it. Usually it is the expense which holds back the sales of exciting cars but the Thunderbird, less special equipment, is approximately £1,200 in its own country and £1,690 here with transportation and other charges added. Alas, purchase tax then adds another £850, and my radio would be a lot extra.   M. A. S.

(Since these personal impressions were recorded, the 1957 model has been announced and a brief description follows.)

NEW CARS DESCRIBED

The 1957 Thunderbird

By ROGER HUNTINGTON, A.S.A.E.

Tidier tail and less shortness on the 1957 T-Bird

BIG styling changes are seen on the Ford Thunderbird for '57 but only minor mechanical modifications. They've tried —and I think they've done a pretty good job—to make this thing a miniature version of about 40 million other American *passenger* cars on the road. Ford doesn't even pretend to call this a sports car any more—they're pushing it as a distinctive "personal" car for business and pleasure use. A comparable model in Britain might be the Bristol. Ford sales people learned early in the project that the big money lay in this sales line; the way the T-Bird is out-selling the Chevrolet Corvette (10 to 1) is proof enough that they were right.

Meanwhile, the Thunderbird grows more and more like the everyday family saloon. For the new model they're boasting, not more performance and better roadability—but 5½in more length, more luggage space, more massive bumpers, exhaust ports in the rear bumpers, transistor radio with automatic volume control, two-tone upholstery, and so on. The final blow will fall early next year when a *four-seat* version is announced.

Mechanically, the new T-Bird has adopted some of the new Ford-Mercury chassis parts—larger brakes, 14in wheels and a new rear axle with lower-slung, straddle-mounted pinion. Last year's 312 cu in V-8 has a hotter cam, slightly higher compression, vacuum-centrifugal spark advance, and can be had in several options rated from 212 to 270 b.h.p. (with twin 4-throat carbs.). Transmission options continue as the 3-speed torque converter (Fordomatic) and 3-speed manual transmission with and without overdrive. Probable performance with 270 b.h.p. is 0-60 m.p.h. 9½ sec, top speed 115 m.p.h.

Bob Veith
TESTS AND COMPARES:
CORVETTE
T-BIRD
GOLDEN

Bob Veith, this month's comparison tester, is one of the fastest-rising stars along the Championship Trail. Last year he drove the Federal Engineering Special to seventh place at Indianapolis and won the coveted Stark & Wetzel Rookie of the Year Award.

This year's versions of Detroit's
hot trio have one thing in common—GO!
Here's how they stack up comparatively.

By BOB VEITH

MY STRONGEST impression after comparison-testing the 1957 Ford Thunderbird, Studebaker Golden Hawk and Chevrolet Corvette is that they're geared for go! All three of these American-built sports-type cars are virtual bombs, loaded with power; yet characterized by individual styling and performance features that set one aside from the other.

I doubt seriously if any of them can be classed as true sports cars for, in most cases, they have been designed to achieve more than one purpose. The Golden Hawk, for instance, obviously was designed for family-car comfort and roominess with sports car performance added. The Thunderbird meets the situation about half-way in each direction. It looks a great deal like a sports car, contains many sports car features, and yet has the soft ride and other features of a family car. As for the Corvette, it undoubtedly has been styled to appeal to sports car enthusiasts, and its designers have gone all out to make the Corvette a true sports car.

In my recent test of these cars, made exclusively for SPEED AGE, I found them all to my liking, with the exception of various individual characteristics which we shall discuss throughout the story. In any case, there is no doubt-ing that each of these cars have been designed to fill a particular purpose, according to the wants of the public.

There were many individual differences on each of our test cars to make a true comparison somewhat difficult, and these things should be kept in mind. The Thunderbird, for instance, was the only one of the three to be equipped with power accessories. It featured Ford's power brakes and steering while the others were standard. Then too, the Bird used in our test had a single four-throat carburetor whereas the Corvette was equipped with twin quads and the Hawk featured a belt-driven McCulloch supercharger which is standard on the '57. In addition, the Bird and Corvette were equipped with automatic transmissions while the Hawk had a stick shift and overdrive.

How did they stack up against each other? Well . . . let's take them apart step by step and see.

Designwise, there hasn't been a great deal of change in any of the three cars over last year's models. Hardly any change at all is noticeable in the appearance of the '57 Corvette over the '56, and the same holds true for the T-Bird; although the latter does boast a slight change to the rear deck and bumper. Hawk body changes include canted tail fins which are a big improvement; louvering of the hood; a bit less chrome stripping; and redesigned tail

HAWK

Corvette shows very little styling
change, but the new power plant is
loaded with high-speed punch.

lights. In each case, the three cars have retained the basic body styles that have become so familiar to today's motorist.

THE CORVETTE

For the out-and-out sports car enthusiast, the '57 Corvette has the best styling and comes closest to filling the bill for a true sports car—even to the simulated wheel hubs, which are most realistic. Bucket seats, stiff shocking, lack of bulky bumpers on both front and rear, plus a moderate use of chrome stripping add a racy look to the car, and give it the feel of a true sports car.

The Corvette is small, with a 102-inch wheelbase and an overall height of 49.2 inches with the convertible soft top down. A removable metal top also is available, which extends the overall height to 51 inches. Twin exhausts, projecting from the rear fenders, offer a pleasant rumble that goes naturally with the car's racy design.

The body is made of fiberglass and is comparatively light. Workmanship seems better than in previous years, but I cannot understand why the designers persisted in using fiberglass for the firewall separating the engine compartment from the cockpit. Any car that is likely to be used in competition, such as the Corvette, should have the safety of a solid metal firewall to protect the driver in the event of trouble.

Fuel injection, of course, is a new feature with the stock Chevrolet as well as the Corvette, and with it the senior engine in the Corvette line boasts one horsepower for each cubic inch of piston displacement. This big engine is listed at 283 cubic inches with an identical horsepower rating. Our test car, however, contained the 245 hp V-8 power plant, equipped with twin four-throat carburetors. A 220 hp engine with single quad carburetion also is available.

Like most sports cars, the Corvette is a bit difficult to get in and out of, especially for a big man like myself, but I soon acquired the knack and didn't have much trouble after awhile. Inside, leg room is surprisingly plentiful and I went for the bucket seats. They seemed to offer me more support, especially to my back and legs. The interior itself is luxurious, with foam rubber cushioning and leather upholstery matched in color with the floor carpeting.

The steering wheel of the Corvette definitely is of sports car design, and sits at a comfortable angle which offers the best possible vision through the wraparound windshield. The seat adjustment, however, is limited. I would suggest an adjustable steering column that would help solve the problem for big fellows like me.

Our test Corvette was equipped with safety belts, but these are optional, as they are on the T-Bird and Golden Hawk. I can't see why belts are not standard equipment,

Front-rear views show T-Bird to be noticeably lower. Continent-style spare mounting has been replaced by trunk stowage, as in earliest models.

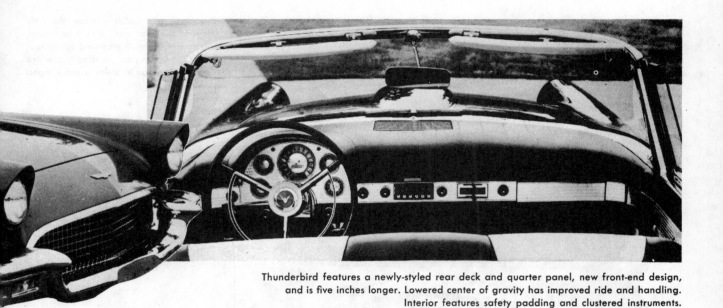

Thunderbird features a newly-styled rear deck and quarter panel, new front-end design, and is five inches longer. Lowered center of gravity has improved ride and handling. Interior features safety padding and clustered instruments.

especially on cars such as these, which are designed for sports-minded enthusiasts. I don't believe the public will ever use seat belts religiously unless the manufacturers push them harder. Many people do use them now, but I'm for making them standard equipment.

While the Corvette was equipped with just about every necessary instrument and gauge, including a tachometer, the instrument panel is not laid out practically. The tach and speedometer can be read without difficulty; but some of the important gauges, such as the oil pressure and ammeter, are strung out far to the right of the driver. I was hunting and taking my eyes off the road for too long a period to see them.

Forward vision out of the wraparound windshield is good; but side vision is restricted with the top up. I found it difficult to see oncoming traffic when pulling onto a main highway from a side road. This problem, of course, does not exist when the top is removed. Unfortunately, our test was made in the rain, so the top was most welcome at the time.

Also in the sports car style is the Corvette's gear shift or selector—a stubby lever located on the floor within easy reach of the driver's right hand. It was no problem to select the proper gear without hunting—a problem I had with the Thunderbird.

As for performance and handling, I could sense the Corvette's power before I even started away from the curb for the first time. It took off with a neck-snapping burst that promised an interesting time in the acceleration runs I was to make later on the drag strip at Long Beach, California.

As mentioned, it was raining when I put the Corvette through its paces; but despite wet pavement it accelerated with tremendous punch. Equipped with a 3.55 gear, we took the car through a series of runs on the drag strip. Surprisingly enough, there wasn't much rear-wheel slippage from the wet pavement during any of the runs. The engine never missed a beat. It seemed willing and capable of taking every bit of throttle I gave it, and the higher the tach went the more punch it delivered. Here are the figures:

0-30	0-40	0-50	0-60	0-90	0-100
2.82	4.24	5.21	6.93	15.50	17.59

From 30 mph on up, the engine seemed to deliver more punch, and continued to do so as the speed soared. Actually there was some slippage at higher speeds, which might have held our 0-100 test down somewhat. But the figures we did come up with are indicative of the wallop the car has. Most of the runs were made in low gear, shifting into drive when necessary on the longer runs. Our figures came out much better this way, since there was a slight miss

noticeable when we tried accelerating in drive range.

These acceleration runs also provide a good brake test since I brought the car to an immediate stop after each run. The best test came from our 0-100 run when I brought the Corvette to a panic stop. There was considerable brake fade under constant usage, but our panic stop wound up without incident.

Handling and cornering, the Corvette was a bit light on the rear end. I took it over a winding course of twisting left and right hand turns running uphill and down. The car handled well, but it seemed stiffer shocked than the '56, and gave a more jarring ride. There wasn't much body lean as I bent it into tight turns, but the back end wanted to get out.

Taking it into a turn, the car felt stable until I began punching the throttle for quick acceleration coming out. Too much punch broke the rear wheels loose from the pavement and caused the back end to sway. When that happened, I was forced to get off the throttle for an instant in order to correct the drift. A bit more weight, perhaps by moving the engine back slightly, might have corrected this.

Steering was about right. It was fast; but not too fast so as to cause oversteering in the turns. Whenever I did get into a slide, a slight turn of the wheel brought me out of it without a lot of effort. Then, too, the engine picked up rpm in a hurry. Much better, in fact, than last year's Corvette. What rpm I lost in backing off to correct a slide was quickly regained, so I didn't lose much time in the corners.

Generally speaking, I'd say that the Corvette has come a long way in the American-built sports car picture since it was first introduced to the public. Its future then was uncertain, but the '57 certainly dispels any doubts that the Corvette is here to stay.

THE THUNDERBIRD

The '57 Thunderbird, although not emphasizing true sports car design to the extreme of the Corvette, carries many sports car characteristics. Like the Corvette, it is small, with a 102-inch wheelbase and a 51.6-inch overall height with removable hard top. But still it carries the comfort and many other features of a passenger car, such as a solid seat and softer shocking.

The T-Bird's bumpers, highly chromed and rather large, are related to a passenger car; but the famous Thunderbird grille work and sculptured rear fins give it the look of a sleek sports model. I thought the fins and grilles really emphasize the Bird's good looks.

Luggage space in the '57 is greater than before, even with the spare tire now located inside. However there is no solid partition between the inside end of the trunk and rear of the seats. With the car's top down, a person could simply open the door, reach behind the seat, and remove whatever was locked in the trunk. The only partition on our test car was a cloth which separated the trunk from the back of the seat.

Like the Corvette, the Thunderbird also has a removable metal top as well as a convertible soft top for foul-

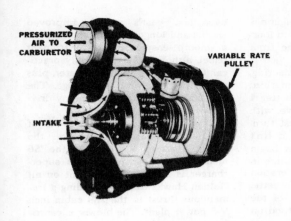

PRESSURIZED AIR TO CARBURETOR

VARIABLE RATE PULLEY

INTAKE

COMPARATIVE SPECIFICATIONS

1957	CORVETTE	T-BIRD	HAWK
ENGINE:			
CYLINDERS	V-8	V-8	V-8
BORE	3.875	3.80	3.56
STROKE	3.00	3.44	3.63
DISPLACE-MENT	283 CU. IN.	312 CU. IN.	289 CU. IN.
COMPRES-SION RATIO	9.5:1	9.7:1	7.8:1
MAXIMUM HP	245 @ 5000	245 @ 4500	275 @ 4800
MAXIMUM TORQUE	300 LB/FT @ 3800	332 LB/FT @ 3200	333 LB/FT @ 3200
CARBURE-TION	TWIN QUADS	SINGLE QUAD	SINGLE DUAL-THROAT W SUPER-CHARGER
HP. PER CUBIC INCH	.866	.788	.951
GEARING:			
TRANSMIS-SION	POWERGLIDE	FORDOMATIC	STICK SHIFT W OVER-DRIVE
REAR	3.55	3.56	3.56
DIMENSIONS:			
WHEELBASE	102 IN.	102 IN.	120.5 IN.
LENGTH-OVERALL	168.01 IN.	181.4 IN.	204 IN.
WIDTH OVERALL	70.46 IN.	72.8 IN.	71.3 IN.
HEIGHT OVERALL	51.09 IN.	51.6 IN.	56.5 IN.
TREAD-FRONT	57 IN.	56 IN.	56.7 IN.
REAR	59 IN.	56 IN.	55.7 IN.
POWER-WEIGHT RATIO:			
WEIGHT	2829 LB.	3372 LB.	3265 LB.
POUNDS/HP	11.54 LB.	13.76 LB.	11.87 LB.
PERFORMANCE:			
TOP SPEED	122.5 MPH.	119.3 MPH.	127.5 MPH
ACCELERATION 0 - 30 MPH	2.82 SEC.	3.65 SEC.	2.63 SEC.
0 - 40	4.24	5.45	3.79
0 - 50	5.21	7.23	5.69
0 - 60	6.93	8.49	7.46
0 - 90	15.50	19.65	16.85
0 - 100	17.59	22.19	23.73

weather driving. Two metal tops, in fact, are available this year. The standard one is fitted with two "port" windows that offer better side vision. The other does not have the port holes and looks more attractive. So you have a choice of a top with better side vision or one that restricts side vision but looks nice.

A true padded dash is one of the finer points of the T-Bird's elaborate interior. Then, too, I liked the clustered instrument panel, hooded from glare and located directly in front of the driver for quick reading. It contained a tachometer, but I was disappointed by the absence of an oil pressure gauge and ammeter. Like passenger cars, the Thunderbird uses red warning lights for oil and battery. I much prefer the others, especially for a sports car design.

Leg room was a bit more cramped than in the Corvette, and I didn't feel quite as comfortable in the solid seat as I did in the bucket type. However I liked the way I could rest my right leg against the gear selector located on the floor. It was a restful position for long drives. The gear selector itself had a lock button located on top of the knob which eliminated the possibility of moving the selector from drive to reverse while in motion. This lock must be depressed before the lever can be moved out of "park" position or into reverse. It is a good point; but a little bothersome to work at times.

Seating position in the Bird is comfortable; but I found the seat adjustment limited, and there's a definite need for an adjustable steering-wheel column. The steering wheel itself is ideally located for comfort and good vision through the wrap-around windshield.

As mentioned, our test Thunderbird was powered by a 312-inch V-8 engine with a single quad carburetor and a horsepower rating of 245. It also had power brakes and steering which ate up some of that horsepower, but made for more comfortable driving. Other power plants available this year are the 312 inch 270 hp V-8 with twin quads, and the 292-inch 212 hp V-8 with a double barrel carburetor. Overdrive also is available with stick transmission. Our test car was equipped with Fordomatic drive, and a 3.56 gear.

Our test car was lively enough on the highway, but did not measure up to the acceleration of the Corvette. This was to be expected because of the difference in carburetion and engine size.

I used low range when possible on each of the acceleration tests, shifting into drive on the longer runs. The times we came up with were not as quick as the Corvette but we weren't exactly standing still, either. Any car that will accelerate from 0-60 in under nine seconds these days is fairly quick. Here are the results of the T-Bird runs:

0-30	0-40	0-50	0-60	0-90	0-100
3.65	5.45	7.23	8.49	19.65	22.19

The take-off response up to 70 mph was neck-snapping all right, and the engine continued to deliver a good punch even on the high end, all things considered. Our time from 0-100 was slow by comparison to the Corvette, but the engine was still revving at the end of our run. This meant it was capable of much more speed before starting to peak out.

Braking was rather severe on the Bird, on panic stops especially. There was noticeable fade under constant use but good recovery. Our power-brake panic stop was even, and we didn't do much fishtailing despite the wet pavement.

For handling and cornering, the Thunderbird gave its competitors a real run for their money. It felt to me the best balanced of the three, with even weight-distribution throughout to make cornering in tight turns a comparatively easy chore. High speed or low speed running, and even on slick pavement, it outhandled the others.

Most impressive was the way it laid into sharp corners. I could take it in hard, begin a desired four-wheel drift, then climb on the throttle and accelerate out of the turn in quick time. Shocking was softer than on the Corvette; but body lean and front-end dive

was hardly noticeable, since weight distribution seemed to allow an even four-wheel drift that kept both the front and back end stable.

I wasn't too keen on power steering, but the more I drove the Thunderbird through winding curves the better I liked it. It is quick and positive, with instant reaction to the slightest turn. Unlike conventional steering, it isn't necessary to lead the wheel or begin the turn before you actually get into it.

Although the Bird's acceleration figures were slower than the Corvette, the 245-hp engine moved out of the turns in a hurry whenever I stood on it during the cornering and handling tests. The power was always there when I needed it.

For the enthusiast who wants more rapid acceleration, the Thunderbird's 270 with dual quads should give him all the punch he wants. In any case, the '57 T-Bird stands to become more popular than ever before. Its soft and comfortable ride, plus its sport-car handling and good looks, are qualities that appeal to any red-blooded motorist.

THE GOLDEN HAWK

I give a lot of credit to Studebaker designers and engineers, who were faced with the problem of coming up with a dual-purpose automobile. It had to be big enough and appealing enough for the family man who also loved sports-car design and features. Their answer was the Golden Hawk.

Unlike the Thunderbird and Corvette, the Hawk was designed to fit a family man's needs as well as those of a sports car advocate. This meant the designing of a bigger and heavier automobile with the punch and looks of a sports model. The '57 Hawk has achieved this purpose with a well-designed five-passenger automobile powered with a 275 hp supercharged V-8 engine that packs a mean wallop.

Supercharging the '57 Hawk is one of the main selling points this year, but there have been other changes, too. The body style, for instance, is greatly improved over last year, with the canted fins, new style taillights and modest chrome stripping. Following the passenger car design, it has a solid roof that is not removable, but still the car has a sporting look about it.

The swept back roof, low silhouette, louvered hood and unmistakable snout-like grille give the Hawk a handsome look, and distinguish it from standard Studebaker models. Like the Corvette and T-Bird, it attracted plenty of attention from passing motorists and pedestrians, who stopped to look it over whenever we parked.

This year's Hawk has a 120.5-inch wheelbase plus new improved-action steering that is a great improvement

over last year's model. Improved shocks and longer springs give the car a smooth, easy ride. The instrument panel, although plain, is highly practical. Gauges include a tachometer, plus an oil pressure and amp gauge. The vacuum gauge helps in economy driving.

The Hawk's engine for '57 is of Studebaker design, and replaces the 275-hp Packard V-8 used in the '56 models. The new Jet Stream supercharger is standard equipment on all Golden Hawks this year, adding a tremendous thrust to the 289 cubin inch V-8 power plant. The blower is centrifugal-type, self-lubricating and comparatively quiet in operation.

Surprisingly enough, the exceptional gas mileage, for which Studebaker has been known, has not been lost with the addition of the blower.

We put the Hawk through acceleration runs over the Long Beach drag strip just as we had the Corvette and T-Bird. There was one difference: we had a dry day for the Hawk test. Our test car contained a 3.56 gear and a stick transmission. It didn't beat the Corvette at high speeds, but from 0-40 mph it was the fastest of the three. Here are those results:

0-30	0-40	0-50	0-60	0-90	0-100
2.63	3.79	5.69	7.46	16.85	23.73

The blower definitely gave the car a tremendous boost on acceleration, especially on the low end, as the comparison figures show. It was very effective up to 70 mph, when it began peaking out slightly. At 90 mph, the rpm really began running out, and we lost considerable elapsed time from 90 to 100. The figures show the Thunderbird, which was slower than the Hawk and Corvette in each of the other acceleration runs, was actually faster than the Hawk from 0-100 mph.

This peaking out at about 90 mph is a problem that the factory has been conscious of for some time now, and a modification that will correct it is being made available. Most of the trouble seems to lie in carburetion—possibly too small a carburetor bowl area. Several Hawk owners have helped the situation by adding an electric booster fuel pump or by installing a smaller carburetor float.

On acceleration, I experienced some rear end chatter caused by the rear wheels breaking traction. As in the Corvette, the rear end was light. Much of the Hawk's weight seems to be concentrated on the front wheels. This was noticeable in cornering and handling tests. I would prefer Traction Masters for more positive rear traction on acceleration, and heavier shocks and springs for handling. Heavy-duty shock absorbers and springs are available for the Hawk this year, as optional.

CONTINUED ON PAGE 53

THREE YEARS OF GLORY

1955 – 1957

Several times during its many decades of automobile production, the Ford Motor Company has developed unique and unusual automobiles, the Model T, Model A, Lincoln Continental, Edsel, Retractable, and the Mustang. But probably the most popular of all among the group was the "Early Birds," the two-seat Thunderbirds of 1955-57. Here is an appreciation of this design concept that burst forth in glory, faded for a time then returned like a Phoenix bird in triumph. Long may the "Early Birds" continue to roll over America's highways.

By Frank Taylor

The 1955 Thunderbird probably should have been called a Phoenix after the legendary bird that rose from its own ashes, for that in essence is what this timeless automobile did. The facts behind the birth of the little Thunderbirds are as unique as the automobiles themselves.

When Henry Ford died, he left behind a shambles at the vast factory that bore his name. Even though no bombs had fallen on the physical facilities, inwardly the sprawling industrial giant lay in ruins. Realizing this, Henry Ford II sought outside help to put Ford back into a competitive position in the domestic and foreign markets it had once ruled.

One of the men to join Ford during this critical time was Lewis D. Crusoe who was soon appointed Ford vice-president and general manager of the Ford Division. Because he was a man of uncommon vision, Crusoe knew that among the things Ford lacked in the early years after WW II was prestige and glamour which in turn would result in publicity and eventually more sales.

Even though the GM dream cars never reached production, they were ideal image builders in auto shows, they stole valuable newspaper space from competitors, and kept the corporate name before the public.

In return, the Ford Motor Company had a fiberglass rear deck lid which the elder Ford once hit with a baseball bat in a publicity still, then promptly forgot, and some other design putterings of small note excluding of course the continentals which were out of production. What was lacking was a dynamic and challenging product that would galvanize attention and excite the public. Somewhere in the back of Crusoe's mind, he was harboring a desire to trample Chevrolet in the sales race and move into number one spot—but what would be the best way to do it?

Crusoe liked to visit auto shows and get the "pulse" of styling trends and public reactions, and the Paris Auto Show was the highlight of such activities in the early 1950's when the Thunderbird first began to germinate as an idea in the mind of Crusoe.

Legend says that in 1951 Crusoe went to the Paris gala and after seeing the many two-seat automobiles on display, decided it might be the ideal way to forge ahead in the sales race, since a small, exciting automobile would grab national attention. There was one other factor which might have prompted him to think along these lines as well.

One of the models on exhibit at the show was GM's LeSabre and it wouldn't have taken much of a crystal ball to determine the influence this particular styling might have in the future on the public taste. GM was likely to steal more customers from the still conservatively styled Ford line unless something dramatic was done.

Deciding to get a jump on his former employer, Crusoe crystalized his thinking around a sports-type car with two seats, something he hoped would have the appeal of one of the cars on exhibit at the Grand Palais. Again, according to legend, Crusoe asked George Walker, then a consultant to Ford of styling, to come up with a car that resembled some of

the snappy foreign cars he had seen.

Walker had won a recent competition against factory stylists when he designed the 1949 models and was anxious to prove himself again. He and his staff plunged into the project quickly. Crusoe understood the need for coordinated efforts in a company as large as Ford, and he was determined to purge this flaw if humanly possible.

The age-old complaint of stylists has been that engineers tend to be dogmatic and ultra conservative, frequently unwilling to make engineering concessions to stylists. Further down the chain of production, were the people who kept track of costs, and finally the salesmen. Salesmen frequently complain about the impractical nature of many automobiles.

It is often one thing to come up with a thrilling design on paper, translate it into metal then roll the finished product on to the showroom floor, only to find out the customers don't want it. The industry has had some bitter experience along these lines. The Chrysler Airflow series, the Mercedes-Benz Gullwings with a wide door sill that made graceful entrance for women almost impossible, and the Darrin sports car with a sliding door that couldn't be locked from the outside.

Crusoe hoped to achieve something more than just a styling triumph and a glamour package with the sports car, he also planned to lay the ground work for future automobile

designs that would affect the future of the Ford Motor Company. The year before his trip to the Paris Auto Show, Crusoe had set up a "product planning" section in order to provide better communication channels along the line of production.

It was probably this development as much as anything else, that helped the Thunderbird come into being as quickly as it did.

A small sports car was on the drawing boards in the studio of Damon Woods in 1951, but when it was decreed 1955 would be the year new sales records would be set, it was decided to pull out all the stops at Ford styling in an effort to produce a product that would smash the competition. The sports car Damon Woods was working on was shelved.

In 1952 new life was breathed into the scuttled sports car project when it was learned that Chevrolet might make such a car. In typical fashion, Ford started a market sampling program to determine if a market existed for a two-seat sports car. About the same time, they contacted dealers to find out if they were enthusiastic about the proposed automobile.

This is something that Hudson had neglected to do when the Italia was introduced. In that case, the factory waited too long to seek dealer opinion and as a result, less than 30 dealers ordered the car. The Italia fizzled and died almost without a chance of success

GRACEFUL BIRD—Many enthusiasts consider the 1957 Thunderbird the most graceful and attractive of the 1955-57 period, and at one time the factory considered resurrecting the body dies from the Budd Company and releasing the automobile again on a Falcon chassis. Instead, however, the Mustang was developed as an alternate proposal and the little Bird "died" a second death.

CAR CLASSICS

mainly because it suffered from poor communication between the factory and the dealers.

Crusoe didn't expect to make that same mistake.

When the first Corvette showed up at the GM Motorama, January, 1953, Crusoe was all eyes. First of all, it was certain in his mind that GM was about to gamble on the concept of a small, sports car, and that they would do it quickly. Unless Ford moved to create something of their own, Chevrolet would steal important thunder in the market place in 1954-55—the very years Crusoe expected to overtake his rival. Clearly it was a time for action.

But there was something else Crusoe noticed, the Chevrolet entry into the field would likely be fiberglass. He smelled a chance to slip in a TKO punch on his rival by using steel in the construction of his sports car—whatever it turned out to be.

What was the car to look like, what were the design objectives, and a thousand other

sporty.

But lest their enthusiasm carry them away, Crusoe dictated some strong terms. The new car was to look like the standard Ford so that potential customers wouldn't be too distracted from big car sales, and those who admired the little car could associate it with the "bread and butter" members of the Ford family. It was a directive that stiffled a lot of wild ideas and made a few of the minor stylists a little bitter, but it proved to be a wise decision.

Corvette on the other hand, opted for a unique appearance, a car that had its own character completely (well almost) separate from the standard Chevrolet products. This was a move they were to regret later, although echoes of the Corvette rearend treatment were seen on the Nomad station wagons in 1956-57. The sales psychology at GM was not as astute as the Crusoe-directed program. Time was to prove Lewis Crusoe something of a market psychic.

the clay were thick and bulky and this made measurements somewhat inaccurate, but the effect of seeing a complete car in toto was dramatic and it saved time. Maguire had also achieved something else, he now had a car that combined an integration of exterior and interior styling. He also had a peculiar Jekyll-Hyde creation with two different side profiles.

GM had adopted the trend for rounded body styles—lines that seemed to flow over the chassis. This was evident in the rear fender treatment of the Corvette, the Cadillac tail fin, and the post 1949 Buick fenders fore and aft. To strike a sharp contrast, Ford had started its modern post-war efforts with an angular belt line in 1949 that ran from headlight to tail light in one long sweep. This agreed with management.

They felt the trend should continue, and even though stylists objected, and even included the "new" rear fender interruption aft of the door jam which was to figure prominently into the styling of other factories, the designers were overruled.

Now a problem of asthetics arose. With the door line dropped to an extra low position, and with only an inch between the trailing edge of the door and the fender cutout, the car looked almost brittle, like it might break in two at the joint. Little could be done to correct this, while management demanded straight, crisp belt lines, so a cop out was used. Fender skirts.

The skirts gave the side profile of the Thunderbird a stronger, more substantial appearance, and this seemed to solve the problem in visual terms at least. A side crease was also added which ran forward to the front fender accenting phoney louvers that were placed midway between the leading edge of the door and the front fender cutout.

While the new body designs were still in the clay forms, a steady stream of visitors came in and out of the shop. Pros and cons were tossed back and forth and almost everyone from Henry Ford II on down trooped in to see the mockup—either on official visits, or often as not, unauthorized "peepers" who wanted to see what the new car might look like.

The Paris Auto Show must have still weighed heavily on the mind of Crusoe because the factory bought several sports cars seen at that display, a Nash-Healey, Jaguar XK-120, and an Aston Martin. At least one man on the payroll at the time also thought a Ferrari was purchased for comparisons, but we haven't been able to confirm this.

Certainly the European cars of that day were rounded, more on the mold of GM products, so it is surprising they were considered at all. One veteran of this period told the author, "I think the foreign cars were selected because they could be measured for interior dimensions, comfort, weight and handling, and visibility, rather than the inspiration that might be gleaned from their exterior skins."

The stylists hung on to the very last, hoping that a decision might be made in favor of their raised "kickup" of the beltline, but about April final word came through, to go with the straight styling approach. Of course, in view of the early directive to keep the Thunderbird's appearance close to that of the big

CHIEF STYLIST—George W. Walker, as Vice President and Director of Styling, did the initial work on Thunderbird, and is given credit for overall design.

questions were set down in firm directives. About February, 1953 final word reached production planners that a new Ford sports car was to be built and a clay model ready by May. It was a tight schedule, but one that all concerned felt they could meet.

A by-product of the enterprise was the feeling that seemed to sweep through the company. For the first time in decades, the work force from the office boys to the front office were inspired with the prospect of exciting Ford automobiles and the firm's first sports car. It was a time of challenge.

The program called for a two-passenger automobile that would use stock components from the full-sized line, plus have a convertible top. It would weigh in at 2500 pounds or slightly more, and use a V-8 engine. Because of the V-8 decision, it was projected the new car would top 100 mph easily, thus appealing to the man who liked to brag about his car's prowess.

Stylists had asked for a chance to move the engine closer to the firewall so that a close-couple look would be achieved, feeling (correctly) that a long hood and shortened rear deck would make the car look dramatic and

With the defined guidelines they were to work under, the various departments leaped into the malestrom that was swirling around the mystery car, while basic styling went to the factory design team, then directed by Bob Maguire.

There wasn't as much latitude in the Thunderbird design as one might have supposed because of the need to make it look like the 1955 car. After all, the basic body shell of the 1955 would be the same one introduced in 1952 with some modifications, so there were a number of limiting factors to be considered by the stylists. It was not going to be an easy project and Crusoe knew it, but he needed a minor styling miracle and it was his intention to wring it out of his men.

Damon Woods was again drawn into the picture and by late February, he had a remarkable clay model in progress. The model had a fully-detailed interior which quickly made it a milestone at that time in clay modeling processes. In previous years, the interior was done separately—often by someone other than the body model department.

There were certain problems attendant to this procedure. The structures used to support

COMPARISION VIEWS—The 1957 when contrasted with the 1958 model, was a dramatic difference, but the popularity of the 1957 version has endured while the so-called "Box Bird" has not.

THUNDERBIRD'S FATHER—Lewis D. Crusoe is considered the father of the Thunderbird, and in many respects is one of the architects of the prestige recovery of the Ford Motor Company. He died in 1973.

"JAYNE MANSFIELD" THUNDERBIRD—This picture has been circulated as a car made for actress Jayne Mansfield, but in actual fact, it was produced for actress Sandra Giles who is shown sitting on the fender. The car was covered with pink, shaggy, acrylic "fur" and the interior was also fixed this way. The car created a sensation wherever it was driven by Miss Giles, but was never owned by Miss Mansfield. Photo courtesy of Ray Miller.

ASSEMBLY LINE—The entire range of the 1955-57 Thunderbirds were given careful detailing by the factory, and the quality that was built in has kept the resale of the cars above a $2,500 average for decades.

STANDARD BIRD—When released, the 1955 Thunderbird was clean-looking, functional in its appointments, and according to most owners, a joy to drive - if the car was equiped with power steering, something most owners added later.

STRONG SIMILARITIES—The 1957 Thunderbird owed much of its handsome stylieg update to its big brother, the Fairlane 500. Of the two vehicles, the Thunderbird came out on top in the styling department.

CAR CLASSICS

Ford, there was never much of a chance anything less would be accepted.

One of the other "rules" at Ford in those pristine days was the "law" that sheet metal ended with the lower edge of the bumper. Corvette might allow the body to flow under the bumper into a neat rounded shape below the grille, Jaguar might do the same, but not Ford. Square cut. Clean cut! Period!!!

Two other factors contributed much to the classic look of the overall design, one was the use of standard head lamp and tail light trim and lenses. The other was the attractive hood scoop. The first was forced (literally) on the designers to cut costs, the latter because of lowered hood line didn't leave enough room to position the motor and still cover it with the hood.

The scoop was added and it was a hit with the public. Function and decoration, a nice combination. The accountants could congratulate themselves on the fact that this time at least, their sharp pencils were mightier than the designers pens. But the accountants weren't through yet. They had found another way to save money, this time on bumpers.

The "donuts" on the front bumpers are raised above the bar. The reason? So they could be punched out and the same unit used for exhaust ports on the rear. Neat.

Heating was to prove a problem, and this came about because the radiator was inclined forward to make room under the hood. A special shroud was then used to allow the fan to function properly from its distant perch on the engine block. Several modifications have been made by 1955-56 Bird owners to overcome the heating problems inherent in this last minute patch job at the factory.

It should be noted here that the designers got their clay mock-up ready for final approval on May 18. The car was "dressed up" for the occasion with tinfoil for the chrome trim and the clay surfaces painted. Last minute corrections were made to the belt line, a round "bump" over the rear wheel was lopped off and an edge so straight it might have been drawn with a T-square was the result.

The early Birds used a heavy-duty rear axle from the station wagon line, and a heavy X-member brace to shore up the somewhat flimsy body panels which had been cut away to almost nothing in places. The body narrowed to a strip barely one-inch wide between the trailing door edge and the rear wheel cut-out—hardly a structural hallmark, and the engineers and designers knew it.

A test chassis was made from a two-door sedan that was sniped down to a 102-inch wheelbase with a liberal application of cutting torch, hacksaw blades and guts. The vehicle looked strange as hell, but it was a practical solution to a chassis of the proper length for testing.

The engine was lowered to a position in the chassis that the new sports car engine and chassis would share. Trouble quickly developed. It was learned that with the motor lower and further back, the front brakes would lock. The coil springs planned for the Bird were softened from the stock tensions required for the larger car, and the rear left springs were made shorter to match up the new engine positioning. The brake problem was solved by making the primary linings of the front drums shorter and narrower.

Ford made another wise decision at this time. While the new car would be fitted with a simple canvas and bow top, it also had roll-up windows. The Corvette when it appeared, confirmed the decision, but they also used a fiberglass hardtop. A squared-off fiberglass lid was quickly designed for the Thunderbird too.

Crusoe understood the American mind. While a few hardy souls liked to hang their arms over the low-slung edge of a sports car

BOLD LIGHT—The 1956 Thunderbird shared the same lamp housings as the 1956 models. Shown here is a model equiped with back-up lights.

door, the wind blasting them in the face with a screaming engine under the hood, alá Jaguar or Ferrari, the vast majority of buyers were more tempted with interior comfort and engine silence under the hood. The steel body helped achieve sound insulation and it was a familiar body material consumers could trust and feel safe in, (not something exotic like fiberglass) and the creature comforts of roll-up windows, a hardtop and several power accessories finished off the package.

In short, it was comfort with a touch of class and dash.

September, 1953 found the men behind the Thunderbird back in Paris, this time comparing the Thunderbird (still without a name) at home with the sleek foreign cars on display. The story goes that Crusoe strolled up and down the aisles of the cavernous building looking closely at everything on exhibit. Finally, he gave the nod. The car was slated for production. A new car was about to be born at Ford.

Because he was hungry for publicity and in truth probably couldn't withhold his enthusiasm for the project and the bombshell he hoped to drop on his competitors, Crusoe decided to commit the car for the February, 1954 auto show in Detroit. Nothing in sheet metal would be available by then, but a fiberglass model could be shown. The date was red lined

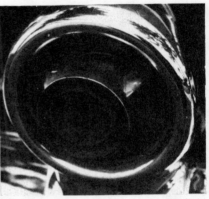

EXHAUST POD—The exhaust pipe exit at the rear of 1955-56 models through "donut" exhaust pods. This same unit was used on the front grill with a chrome center covering the hole.

on executive calendars while the design boys went to work finishing the fiberglass body.

When pictures were taken of the new car for pre-show publicity, a tiny name plate was fastened on it, "Fairlane." This was the name of the Ford home in Michigan, and it had never appeared on a Ford automobile before, but it was less than stunning in its application to the mystery car.

There had been plenty of suggestions. Crusoe was credited with the name Savile, which had a European flavor, others came up with names like El Tigre, Coronado which had a Spanish flavor. One of the members of the staff was from the southwest and he suggested the legendary Thunderbird. This name was a hit among most of those who heard it, but the hunt continued.

There was Sportsman, Sportliner, Runabout (ugh), Arcturus and the previously mentioned Fairlane, but Thunderbird seemed to fit the car the best. The man given credit for the name was Alden R. "Gib" Gilberson, a young stylist at the time who was acquainted with the legends surrounding the Thunderbird. He was later awarded a prize by Crusoe in the form of a custom made, $250 suit which he never had made.

A near disaster resulted when it was learned that GM was also planning to call a car Thunderbird, but Ford beat them to the punch with a fast registration of the name and publicity releases. GM later brought out their car, but re-named it "Firebird," instead.

PEEK-A-BOO SPEEDOMETER—

The stock speedometer from the full-size Ford line was used in the Thunderbird as a cost cutting measure.

Bodies were built by the Budd Company, frames came from A.O. Smith a major supplier, and the hardtops from Mitchel-Bentley. Some of the early Fairlane Fords used gawdy chromed headlight rims, and for a time it looked as though the Thunderbird might suffer this indignity too, but at last reason prevailed and the cars used painted rims.

Probably elated by his success up to this point, Crusoe decided that the chrome spears plastered on the sides of the big Fords should also be attached to the Thunderbird. This time, the stylists dug in their heels. Tooling was let for the trim, some photos were sent out and one or two ads appeared in magazines, but the flying toothpicks were never installed.

A set was saved for Crusoe's personal Bird, and this would be a genuine mini classic of special interest cars if it were ever found. Perhaps it has been located and we just aren't aware of it.

Some how, in light of its successful flight from a near death on the drawing boards, it seems as though the car should have been called a "Phoenix" instead of Thunderbird.

On December 9, 1954 the first of the new Thunderbirds rolled off the assembly line and a new page of history was written for the Ford Motor Company. In the second part of this series we will explore the development of the "personal car" concept, the success of the 1956-57 season and the demise of the little Birds in favor of more lumbering, but commercially successful "Box Birds."

From the moment production started, there was no problem selling the new cars. There are several examples of the 1955 Thunderbird selling for $2,800, but more often, the price was closer to $3,500 per unit when enough options could be obtained. Base price was supposed to be $2,695.

The usual option was the automatic transmission, but more than one owner was content to wait until he was able to get power steering, power brakes, power windows, and other goodies not commonly available in the first months of production. Those who took their cars without power steering lived to regret it.

The steering was both heavy, and when parking, downright tough, but on the road it was so good, one owner said the car almost steered itself. Dealers were soon getting requests for after market power steering units and many did a brisk business in this single feature, although it was no easy job to convert a Thunderbird from manual to power steering.

Another woe that turned up early was heating problems. This was suspected early in the game, but there didn't seem to be time enough to make the changes necessary, and it was the dealers who caught hell when irate owners tried driving their new cars in the hot summer months.

Anyone lucky enough to get air conditioning was soon sorry. Coupled with an automatic transmission and air conditioning, the 1955-57 Thunderbirds got hot, and fast. One of the "no-no's" an owner soon learned was not to sit for any period of time with the car running at an idle. This practice sent the temperature gauges soaring, and this in turn

would rupture the high pressure radiators, blow hoses and probably the drivers mind.

Even on long trips with a fairly high, highway speed, the heating woes continued, but it was in the Western deserts that drivers suffered the most. Arizona, New Mexico, Nevada and parts of Western Texas were places a Thunderbird owner didn't go in his 1955-56 automobile, at least in the summer time.

But these were minor problems, and in some cases, they could be overcome. Clever owners put larger radiator cores in their 'Birds, installed transmission oil coolers, and other tricks that helped the situation, but never really cured it.

As with everything else, there were owners who had no trouble at all, (or if they did have trouble, they didn't talk about it) and reported complete satisfaction with their automobiles. One problem that owners reported to dealers that eventually filtered back to the factory was the heat in the passenger compartment and lack of proper ventilation.

This was a sore point with owners in Southern California, and this was a big sales area for the Ford Motor Company, (in fact, it still is). To solve the problem quickly, a small side

POSH INTERIOR—The Thunderbird interior was both attractive and roomy. The use of a phoney engine turned trim inside was a modern touch that seemed to come off very well.

vent was put on the 1956-7 models, but the 1955 owners had to go on suffering. Another problem that was quickly apparent was poor vision when looking out the left rear of the car.

With the hardtop on, a blind spot is created, and again, the buyers in Southern California seem to have been the most vocal in complaint. When word of this reached Detroit, there was a flurry of activity in the design department to find out how to cure the problem. Help on this problem also came from another quarter. Lewis D. Crusoe was also delighted with his Thunderbird—except for the same deficiency.

This added pressure resulted in a top with quarter panel windows. This solution didn't seem to be the answer, so it was decided that a small round window or porthole should be installed on the top. This satisfied the design department, but not the dealers.

Dealers either liked the idea or they didn't. There didn't seem to be any middle ground. To decide what should be done, the porthole was offered on the 1956-7 models at the same price. It was a good idea, and three of every four Thunderbirds that left the factory after the new window was offered, had the windows.

Around the factory, people were calling the

Thunderbird a "personal car," because of the two-passenger arrangement, and this concept seemed to be shared with the Corvette After we saw the Thunderbird, and rapped the steel fenders a few times, we bought one." The square, plain styling also appealed to most buyers. Another owner explained: "The car seemed to have integrity written all over it, it seemed like a square, on-the-level car, know what I mean?"

Others objected to the "sporty" look of the Corvette. One banker sniffed: "I couldn't drive to work in a Corvette, my customers would have thought I was a hot rodder. But almost everyone wanted a Thunderbird, even if they could afford one."

But on the road, the 1955-57 Thunderbirds without a Continental kit, were no slouch in the performance department. In fact, the idea of the sports car Thunderbird was in the back of the mind of most buyers. They liked the idea of romping on the gas and feeling the car surge ahead, or trying to whip it through a tight corner, (which often accounted for the high insurance rates that were quickly applied to the Thunderbirds) with a howl of low pressure tires.

The car could go, but didn't look like a "hot rod" so it seemed to be the ideal combination for a young executive and his bride or an older businessman and his wife whose kids had builders, except they had gone the route of high power and racy looks.

The early decision to use steel instead of fiberglass probably sealed the success of the 1955-57 Thunderbird over its rival. Most of the original Thunderbird owners we have talked to, shared a common opinion, they didn't like or didn't trust fiberglass.

One man explained: "I didn't even drive the Corvette. I didn't know anything about fiberglass, and I didn't want a car made out of it. grown up. But what about the affluent group with one or two kids, or the couples who liked to take friends on a short trip or to some social function?

Crusoe had his eye on sales figures, and even though the little Thunderbird was selling as fast as they could be produced, he knew that it would be a limited market unless he could add another seat. So in early 1955 plans were already being laid to phase out the one-seat concept in favor of two.

The 1956 Thunderbird was the first one offered with the so-called "Continental kit," and it proved to be a millstone in more ways than one.

The kit was received with a degree of trepidation by engineers who were already having steering problems with the 1955-6 cars. The steering on the 1955 Thunderbird was quick, and coupled with a fairly short, semi-stiff set of leaf springs in the rear, tended to respond quickly. The general reaction to this was not especially good. Few drivers in 1955 wanted a sports car type quick steering.

To compensate, Ford engineers had to do something quick and simple. Redesigning the suspension was out, so was heavy modifications to it. With their options squeezed by such restrictions, the men with slide rules turned to the rear springs. In the 1955 models, there were five-leaves, 48-inches long. One leaf was removed and the springs lengthened to 56-inches.

With the new Continental kit in place and its attendant 350-pounds of overhang, the 1956 Thunderbird was smooth riding, but it also had a distinct wallow. The car seemed separated from the rear section because of the action of soft springs and overhang when cornering or doing much more than going in a straight line.

The 1955 models also suffered from lack of "feel" in the steering. At least one harsh critic of the car felt this was a nearly lethal failing, especially among drivers who had previously been used to muscling a sponge suspended, coil spring sedan through a corner. Drivers of the big touring sedans who switched to Thunderbird found themselves cranking the wheel 4.75 turns lock to lock instead of the 1955 ratio of 3.5, which was closer to full-size car ratios.

The steering ratio change was a last minute attempt to neutralize the faster steering of the first Thunderbird, and compensate at least to a small degree, the effect of the new Continental kit. The kit, like the porthole were mixed blessing many buyers felt. The kit allowed more trunk room, (which is what the engineers were trying to do) and some felt it also added beauty to the overall design—others didn't.

Some test drivers who had compared them, felt the 1956 Thunderbird actually handled better. Still handling was a mute question, and one that each individual driver had to settle for himself, once he got behind the wheel.

As one critic put it, "The (1965) Thunderbird is no sports car. It is best suited for straight-line running and drag racing, if performance, not handling is your interest when you buy one."

Probably the happiest of all were dealers, because the new kit, tail light trim, vent, power option and porthole made the 1955 models look a bit old, and dealers were in the business of selling new cars, so it was a welcome modification for them.

The engine department wasn't neglected either. The first engine had been the so-called "Y-block" V-8 with 292-cubic inches. The standard shift models used an engine rated at 193 hp, while automatics got a 198 hp version. To get the extra thunder, the compression ratio of the automatic engine was raised .4.

To handle the engine power, the 1955 models were fitted with 3.73 read ends for standard shift, 3.92 for overdrive, and 3.31 for automatics. But by 1956, things had changed. Corvette was pushing the power image of its car, and Ford was watching public reaction closely. Again, the engineers took the stock product and made such modifications as they were allowed under cost considerations, to boost the engine output.

The old "Y-block" was bored and stroked (something performance fans had already done with their 1955 cars) to 312 cubic inches. A new head design was used which incorporated bigger valves. A Holley carb was tossed in for good measure with a husky four-barrel throat. All this gave the "new" engine a 215 rating with a standard transmission and 225 with an automatic.

The old 292 was retained for those who satisfied with a little less performance, while

the new engine package became the power option for those who might want to go off against a Corvette at the stop light, (but even with the power package, it wasn't advised). The old engine was given a rating of 202 hp, for 1956, and the rear end ratios stayed the same as 1955.

Acceleration was considered excellent, and many drive reports lavish in their praise of this attribute. A healthy power-to-weight ratio had been maintained which at least kept it in the ball park with Corvette in impromptu drag contests, providing all facts were generally equal. There was a flaw in fast acceleration, however, violent wheelspin because the 1956 Thunderbird still didn't have enough weight on the rear axle—even with the Continental kit.

Tight cornering was a different situation. The 1956 Thunderbird could move through a tight corner with an experienced driver very well, but tended to go "soft" at high speeds in long, sloping corners with inexperienced drivers leaving long skid marks behind. Top speed was improved, with a published report of one run after a five-mile approach at 119.4 mph which wasn't even close to the 150 mph speedometer the factory installed.

Brakes were nothing to write about, most published reports indicate, and drivers who bought the 1956 cars now recall a certain amount of problems over 60 mph. Still, they stopped the car, and until they were trod on constantly, seemed to hold up.

Taken as a whole, the 1956 Thunderbird was an interesting car that filled a dual function. It was small and fast, it was comfortable and good looking, both of which were rules laid down early in the game by Crusoe. But even as the 1956 production run was gearing up for more than 15,000 units, (16,155 were produced) the seeds of an early death had already been planted.

The car would go another year, with a major modification to the body lines in conformance with the major body changes in the 1957 Ford cars, but it would then vanish as a two-passenger version with one seat to emerge as a four-passenger, greatly enlarged automobile. Gone were the lean, hard, size and looks, in was the bulky, flamboyant styling of the late 1950's.

A new era was about to dawn for the Thunderbird, and 1957 would be the watershed year of change.

The 1957 Thunderbird was a happy memory when the Ford Motor Company under the direction of Lee Iacoca decided to think in terms of bringing out a new small car to replace it. The Falcon was in production and the public acceptance of it was strong, but sensing that what was needed was a new product, something with the classic "feel" of the two-seat Thunderbird, Iacoca started considering his options.

Tom Case one of the original "birdmen" was called in and told to find out if the Budd Company still had the original body dies for the 1955-57 Thunderbird, and if they still existed, how much would it cost to revise them and put the car back into production. The assignment thrilled Case because he was a confirmed enthusiast of the original cars. When he called the Budd Company, he was told the dies still existed. Excited by the

prospects of a revival of the car, Budd officials promised to investigate the potential use of the dies, and costs of revision, and other factors. This was the best news of all. No expensive re-tooling would be needed, the car might not be dead after all.

Budd Company set out immediately to create a prototype automobile that could be shown to the Ford officials for approval or modification if it was needed. They proved to be very innovative in their use of existing body stampings and the Falcon chassis it was proposed to mount the new car on.

For identification, the Budd Company labeled the project, XT-BIRD, a pun if there ever was one. The Ford Motor Company uses Budd-built bodies if the run planned is less than 100,000 units. More than that and they build their own. Once more, the Thunderbird was projected as a low run car, so it seemed likely the new car would be made by Budd as had the previous cars.

In anticipation of this, planning at Budd incorporated projections of the new car, and its impact on their production. All of this was expensive, but officials in both companies felt it would be worth the effort. When the new concept was ready, a special booklet was prepared for those concerned with the project, and the new car was unveiled.

Pleased with the results of the combined firms, Lee Iacoca carefully considered the whole idea of the Thunderbird revival and the potential sales impact as well as the implications it might have overall on the entire range of Ford products. The idea of bringing the car back from the dead as it were appealed to many at Ford, including Tom Case who felt it would be an ideal vindication of a classic design and a hot selling car.

Budd Company officials also felt the same way, and had gone to considerable lengths to prove their theories. Newspaper want ad columns were carefully searched, and representative ads were taken from a number of large circulation, metropolitan dailies which showed the asking price of various Thunderbirds from 1955-57 that were being offered for sale.

One particularly graphic example was taken from the New York *TIMES* for December 5, 1961. In this paper it was found that a 1955 Thunderbird, six-years-old was being offered for $1,450. A 1956 model was being offered at $1,700 and a 1957 version had the highest price tag of all, $1,975. In the same

ORIGINAL CLASSICS—
The 1955 Thunderbird was the vindication of Lewis Crusoe's market wisdom and vision which combined basic parts of the full-sized Fords into a compact sports car with a personality all of its own.

paper, Budd gleefully noted that a 1955 Cadillac was listed at $525, a 1956 Cadillac at $900 and a 1957 convertible for $1,200.

The marketing/research team at Budd gloated a bit when they told the Ford people:

"A comparison of these prices with those quoted in the same newspaper for Cadillac Convertibles of the same years, is revealing, particularly in view of the much higher new car cost of the Cadillac. . . .

"What is the reason for this highly unusual used car price situation? Demand for the early T-birds obviously greatly exceeds the supply."

Budd found other indicators of the need for a Thunderbird two-passenger revival besides the want ads, and their conclusions made a lot of sense. Turning to the soaring import statistics as found in automobile registrations, they discovered as of July 31, 1961 total imported two-seat cars in the U.S. was 249,301. Delving further, they found that the MG at $2,444 and the Austin-Healey at $3,051 represented the largest percentage of sales.

In this same price range on the American market there was nothing available in 1961, the Corvette (beep) was the only two-seat car then built and its base price pushed it out of consideration in the $2,500-$3,100 price range. Obviously, if the marketing research of Budd was correct, the American public was buying large numbers of imported sports cars in the $2,500-$3,100 range, and would probably buy an American product just as quickly —if it had a two passenger body style—something that matched the projected Thunderbird price and body style.

But Budd still had more ammunition to fire off. They engaged a firm to conduct a limited, but as they described it, scientifically planned research project to search out public reaction to the new version of the Thunderbird. An artist's sketch was shown to a sampling of 277 persons. Included were housewives, business and professional men, college students, etc., anyone in fact, they felt might influence sales of the car later on, once it was in production.

After seeing the rendering, those contacted during the survey were asked two questions: "What do you think of it?" and "If this car sold for $2,800 would you buy it?"

The responses were good. To the first question, 212 people or 76.5% said yes or something equivalent, with only 65 or 23.5% giving an unfavorable or indifferent response to the question. The second question showed an equally good general response. 108 persons, or more than 50% were "interested," or "very interested" in the new car.

To sum up everything, Budd said:

". . .We believe it can be said with confidence that there is a ready-and-waiting market for a two-seater such as the XT-Bird. We want very much to build this body for you. We feel strongly that the *Ford Motor Company* can capitalize on the marvelous reputation and built-in acceptance of the Thunderbird concept in a market that has evidenced its interest in a sporty roadster—in a market that grows continually larger.

"A car of this type can be built at very low initial tooling cost, to sell—due to its use of high production components—at a popular price. We know this car would be fun to own, fun to drive, and we think it would be fun to sell. . ."

A careful study of the Budd proposal shows that it was sound in all respects, and that it was not an attempted "snow job" on Ford officials, who it must be remembered, had initiated the project in the beginning.

In a brief four months, Budd, working in close cooperation with Ford, had built a full-size prototype (which still exists) and conducted marketing surveys, engineering studies, and even contacted material suppliers relative to the production of the two-seat revival of the Thunderbird. They were convinced as were many people at Ford, that the "new" XT-Bird would have a better market reception, and higher potential sales than it had in 1955 when it was introduced to the public as a brand new Ford product.

After a series of meetings during the summer of 1961, it was decided that the best way to proceed with the XT-Bird project would be to build a car in sheet metal, and thus test their theories. A 1961 Falcon and a 1957 Thunderbird were purchased and by September of that year, work was underway. Budd mobilized its resources, calling upon its design, engineering, production and sales personnel for the effort to create the proper climate for a revised Thunderbird.

While work progressed on the actual prototype and its problems, the sales department conducted the previously mentioned surveys and studies to buttress the general theme of the car and its place in the nation's market place. Budd was fortunate in two respects with the XT-Bird project. The original cars had been a separate body and chassis unit, and the 1961 Falcon was also constructed the same way. The second advantage was the similar wheelbase measurements and identical tread of the two cars.

The Falcon body was removed by Budd engineers, and immediately portions of it were cut off to accomodate the new body. Modifications necessary for the "mating" were surprisingly few. One of the major revisions was removal of the steering column, gas filler neck and some of the support sheet metal flanking the radiator and engine compartment. The firewall was trimmed in height, but little else was needed.

The 1957 Thunderbird was also undergoing a similar process. The major modifications executed on the existing body was to gently curve the front and rear fender lines in a smooth arc which closely conformed with styling trends of the time. The sketches that accompany this article show how this was accomplished with a minimum of cost in revising the original body dies.

Things were humming at Budd as its extensive staff was kept busy solving the multitudes of problems, large and small, that kept cropping up during the revision of the body and chassis components. The "dog leg" windshield curve that had cracked countless kneecaps on the original Thunderbirds, was removed and the windshield redesigned.

Because of the longer Falcon wheelbase, another problem of the early "Birds" was resolved, that of the narrow strip of metal between the rear edge of the door and the wheel cutouts. On the XT-Bird, this space was lengthened and the overall body was thereby strengthened. Fender skirts were retained, but the air scoop on the hood was dropped.

Two other plus factors for the new concept were improved—frontal visibility due to the lowering of the fender lines, and improved rear visibility for the same reasons.

The longer wheelbase also gave the car a better ride, and had the Continental kit been used on it, the handling difficulties of the 1957 models would have been eliminated as

RESURRECTED BIRD—
In 1963, this Thunderbird was created for approval by Lee Iacocca, but only one was made by the Budd Company. Instead of a revived Thunderbird, Iacocca decided to build the Mustang. This car still exists.

well. In overall measurements, the "new" Thunderbird had the exact measurements as its parent, but better use was made of the chassis than in previous years.

The major accomplishment of the Budd creation was the addition of an extra bench seat for packages, midgets or small children, a feature completely lacking in the 1955-57 product line of Thunderbird. While the additional space which resulted in the new positioning of the rear axle was cramped, it was there, and would have added several points to the sales appeal of the new car, especially to families with one or two small children. The engineers were learning from the mistakes of previous history.

But as neatly as the new package came together, there were still a few rough spots to be ironed out. A list was drawn up of the new or revised parts that Ford would supply for the projected body construction. Note how many of the original parts were to be interchangeable with the new car.

The following parts were on the Ford list: Front Bumper, Bracket Assembly, Occasional Seat Finish Moulding, Vent Window Assembly, Windshield Lower Outside & Inside Finish Moulding, Windshield Side Outside & Inside Finish Moulding.

For Budd the new or revised parts would be as follows:

Underbody Side Sills, Underbody Crossmembers, Occasional Seat Back Panel & Parts, Gas Tank Filler Neck, Rear Stone Shield Parts, Radiator Support & Front Fender Apron, Dash, Gear Shift, Windshield Frame Body Parts, Door Vent Window Parts.

There were several good reasons for the new Thunderbird to appeal to the executives at Ford who had some of the sharpest pencils in the industry when it came to cutting costs. The total estimated cost of production for

CAR CLASSICS